THE MAKING OF AN UNSHAKABLE CHARACTER

Daily Lessons To Build Your Life On

Compiled by

Sam Glenn
President, Motivational Presentations

Published by **Sam Glenn, Motivational Presentations**
608 S Washington Ste 101
Naperville, IL 60540
800-818-6378

Additional copies of this book can be obtained from any of the
authors. Also available at:

www.SamGlenn.com

Table of Contents

INTRODUCTION

The purpose of this book is to share the qualities of a solid character. The examples, stories and daily challenges are set before you to help you grow into a man or woman of unshakable character. I once heard a saying that you cannot pour the foundation of a building on the twentieth floor. If you do, the building won't stand. The same is true with character. Your life won't stand if you don't invest in yourself by defining and growing in your character. We may not be able to change many things about the world, but we can change our choices and the way we live. It is my hope that in the next few pages you will find the words that will stimulate you to stand up and step forth.

To create a better life, you must create a better you. This begins with a choice, backed with commitment. Are you worth it? Yes you are. It's the truth. *You need to believe you're worth it from this point on.*

Studies have been conducted regarding character and its impact on success. These studies indicate that fifteen percent of success on the job and in life is based on technical skills and abilities. The studies go on to show that eighty-five percent of your success is based on the person you are, your character.

My challenge to you:

Challenges help us to grow, so I want to challenge you every day to grow in your character. It takes work, determination, practice, the right company and a desire to change, grow, learn and become. I want to challenge you to take **FIVE MINUTES** a day, only five, and commit those precious moments to learning about character. I also challenge you to act on the daily challenge at the end of each lesson by answering the questions and applying what you learn to your life immediately. If you choose to accept the challenges laid out in this book, I promise that your life will change for the better.

CHARACTER QUIZ

Do This Before You Begin This Book.

Circle the answer that best describes your response. Use the answer key to determine how your character rates.

1. Your friend comes up to you and tells you that he and a classmate got into a huge argument.

A. You go directly to the classmate and chew him out.

B. You get both sides of the story and then decide who is right so you can take a side.

C. You tell your friend that you want to be there for him, but the argument does not involve you and you don't want to take sides

2. You want to be the student body president, but every other year you have run for office, you lost the race.

A. You run for office and give it everything you've got. Why not learn from previous years and make the campaign better than ever? Who knows? You may just win!

B. You decide not to run. You never won before, why would you win now?

C. You run for office, but pretend you don't care if you win or lose. You tell people, "I just want to keep with tradition."

3. Your friends are all going to a rave and your best friend's parents are out of town. You know you can tell your parents you are going to your best friend's house and get away with going to the rave, but you know that going to a rave can lead to big trouble.

    A. You go to the rave and tell your parents you are spending the night with your best friend. Why not? You only live once!

    B. You tell your friends that you are not going because you don't want to lie to your parents and raves usually have drugs, alcohol and other things that you don't want to be involved with.

    C. Since you are worried, you call your friends that night and tell them you are very sick.

4. You catch your sister smoking. She begs you not to tell your parents.

    A. You run straight to your parents and tell them. Finally your sister will be busted instead of you.

    B. You promise not to tell and keep your promise.

    C. You tell your sister that you care about her health and that she needs to stop. Tell her that you won't tell your parents if she quits immediately.

5. You and your significant other have been together for several months. You are both going farther and farther physically. You are worried that the next time you will have sex and you are not ready for that.

    A. You continue to put yourself in different situations that make it possible to get physical with your significant other, like an empty house or a secluded road in a car. Why not? You can draw the line.

B. You discuss your feelings with your significant other and together you make a list of physical boundaries and how you will both stick to them.

C. Every time you are alone with your significant other, you try to avoid the situation by making an excuse that you have to leave.

6. You are in class and your teacher unfairly accuses you of talking, when you were not.

A. You roll your eyes and make it obvious to your classmates that your teacher has no clue about anything.

B. You keep quiet and respectfully approach your teacher after class.

C. You immediately respond to your teacher by telling him where to go.

7. You are driving and a person cuts you off the road.

A. You flip him off, honk your horn and yell. How dare him?

B. You get mad and it ruins your day.

C. You blow it off. There are way more important things in life where you can channel your energy.

8. You are hoping your mom will forget that it is your turn to do the dishes.

A. You go ahead do them without being asked. It is your turn.

B. You wait until your mom tells you to do the dishes and then you do them.

C. You wait until your mom tells you to do the dishes. You complain and she has to keep asking you. When you finally do them, you gripe the whole time.

9. You promised several months ago that you would take your little sister to a boy band concert. She is excited to go with you rather than your mom. You just found out your school is going to the state championship game for football that same night.

A. You take your sister to the concert and have a great time. A promise is a promise.

B. You tell your mom that you can't go because you have to fill in for the mascot and there is no one else to do it. (Or some other lame excuse like that.) This is the game of the year! You can't miss it!

C. You take your sister and make sure she knows what a sacrifice you are making and you both have a miserable time.

10. You are backing out your car and you scrape up against a sign. There are scratches all along the side of your car.

A. You try to cover the scratches up so your parents don't notice.

B. You tell your parents exactly what happened.

C. You tell them that you came out to the car and the scratches were just there.

Answer Key

Give yourself points according to the answers that you circled. Add your score and see how your character rates.

1. a) 1   b) 2   c) 3

A person of character does not take up the offenses of others. When two friends are in an argument, the best thing to do is stay out of it, but encourage them to resolve the problem immediately.

2. a) 3   b) 1   c) 2

A person of character perseveres and never gives up. Abraham Lincoln ran for office eleven times before winning a race.

3. a) 1   b) 3   c) 2

A person of character is truthful, even when he/she doesn't have to be. A person of character isn't afraid to lose friends when standing up for what is right.

4. a) 2   b) 1   c) 3

A person of character is not out to make others look bad. A person of character keeps promises, but in a case where someone is at risk, a promise like that should not be made. A person of character is understanding to others, but will take a stand against something that is unhealthy.

5. a) 1   b) 3   c) 2

A person of character communicates his feelings with others and finds solutions. A person of character does not avoid confrontation and communication, nor does he put himself in situations where he could compromise his integrity.

6. a) 2   b) 1   c) 3

A person of character shows respect to authority and knows how to approach a person in a respectful way, when unfairly accused.

7. a) 1   b) 2   c) 3

A person of character knows how to discern what issues to put his energy into and what he should "blow off."

8. a) 3 b) 2 c) 1

A person of character is responsible and takes initiative. A person of character does not have to be asked to do something that is expected of him and he definitely does not complain!

9. a) 3 b) 1 c) 2

A person of character keeps a promise. When a person of character is generous with his time and even though he is missing out on something he would like to be, he makes the best of the situation.

10. a) 2 b) 3 c) 1

A person of character is honest and can humble himself to tell the truth. A person of character does not lie or try to cover up mistakes.

POINTS

25 – 30 points

An Unshakable Character

You are well on the road of making an unshakable character. You consider what is right over what is popular and are more concerned about doing right than what your friends think. While you want to be your best, you look out for the interest of others. You have a solid foundation to build a successful life upon. This book will help you build on your foundation.

20 – 24 points

A Sometimes Shaky Character

You have made many wise choices, but at times you worry more about yourself and what other people think over doing what is right. At times you think through the consequences and about others before you make a decision, but sometimes you only think about what you want. This book will help you be more consistent in the choices you make regarding character.

0 – 19 points

One Shaky Character

While you show some display of character, you have trouble basing most of your decisions on character. Most times, you worry about yourself and what others think rather than making a decision based off what is right. This book will help you build a solid foundation so you can be on your way to making an unshakable character.

SECTION ONE

What is Character?

Day 1

WHAT IS CHARACTER?

Sam Glenn

Reputation is what folks think you are.
Personality is what you seem to be.
Character is what you really are.

Before us lies two paths – only one is paved with character. The wise embark on the path of character; the ignorant and uncaring journey on the other. If you walk the road of character with integrity, you will never have to look over your shoulder.

Before we dive into developing character, we need to define what character is. Without knowing this, we aren't going anywhere. This awareness alone will point you in the right direction, but it is up to you to walk the path of character. As you read about what character is, think about where you are in character development and if you need improvement or need to change something about your present character.

Character is the core of who you are. Character starts on the inside and affects our lives on the outside. It is what you do, the way you live, how you treat others, the way you respond, the way you work, and the choices you make. It's everything you are. It's who you are in private when nobody is looking. Character is what governs your life. It is not compromising or trying to justify a wrong to make it a right. It is not saying one thing and doing another. It's more than knowing right from wrong. It is acting on the principle of what is right and wrong. People of character live with nothing to hide and nothing to prove. They walk with

3

freedom and security. They think before they act, practice self-control in frustrating situations, walk their talk, are trusted by others and are honest in the little things. They persevere in tough times instead of displaying destructive behavior or giving up. They seek the wisdom of others and apply it in their daily lives. They are not superficial. They are real. What you see is what you get. They make life count to the fullest. They are not perfect, but are willing to improve in all areas of life. They are not out to hurt others or display rage when things are unfair. They value themselves and others. They don't just talk about character, they live it! Can this be you - yes it can!

CHARACTER in simple terms is your behavior.
- Character is living your life by a standard, by principles over feelings.
- *"Character is doing what we ought to do, whether we feel like it or not, even when no one is looking."* - Character Training Institute

INTEGRITY IS...
- Not compromising what is right
- Not cutting corners in life

A PERSON OF CHARACTER...
- Can be trusted
- Is real
- Is consistent
- Treats others with respect
- Follows through with commitments

QUALITIES THAT MAKE UP A PERSON OF CHARACTER...
- Perseverance to achieve
- A positive attitude

- The ability and desire to make wise choices
- Openness to change
- Enthusiasm
- A healthy self-image
- Willingness to learn
- Good sense of humor
- Maintains a balanced life
- Cares about others

You have to be willing to evaluate your character. You may or may not be pleased with what you discover about yourself. Ask others if they think you are a person of character.

Maintaining Your Character

Like a car that needs a checkup, oil change, a wash or tune-up, we need to do the same for our character. Character is the core of who we are. It will determine our degree of success in life.

A character tune-up involves...
- Daily attention
- Daily commitment
- Awareness of consequences
- Self-respect

Daily Challenge:
1. Do a personal evaluation. Write a description of the person you think you are.
2. Write a description of the person you really want to be.
3. What would you like to improve about your character?

Day 2

CHARACTER IS A CHOICE

Sam Glenn

"Character is a choice. Choose wisely.
For your choices will determine where you go, what you get,
who you become, and the life you live." – S. Glenn

As you journey the path of life, you learn what is right and wrong, good and bad and in the process we act on this power called choices. We can think, plan, create, love, hate, build, destroy, or help. We can be happy, sad, or hurt. The list of choices we can make is practically endless.

In life, every step we take is a choice we make.
Life is all about choices…Character is a choice.

When I was growing up I was not taught the value or importance of developing a solid character. I barely ever heard the term used. So, when life hit me with challenges or situations, I crumbled, or responded in a way that had negative consequences. I became a product of my environment. I knew the basics of "right" and "wrong", but the emphasis of "why" was lacking. I was not aware of the consequences to my choices. I admit that I carried a below par character into adulthood and sadly there are more like me out there. Tons more. I am thankful for the realization, that with great effort, developing my character has changed my life dramatically.

Instead of learning what "real" character is and taking the time to develop it, many of us claim our own standards and values in life. The problem is that our standard may not be right. It may not benefit your destiny or others around you. Your personal claim to your own standard may be off the mark. This book is geared to help you hit the mark. You will learn the benefits and value to having an unshakable character.

You may have made some mistakes in your past, but today I offer you a fresh start. I offer you the opportunity to walk with me and grow in ways that you have never imagined. Is it really possible to live a fulfilled and rewarding life? Yes! Can I really get ahead in life with honesty, integrity, respect, and solid moral ethics? Absolutely!

I want you to imagine for a moment that you are getting ready to build the house of your dreams. Now you don't want this house to cave in on you while you're sleeping, or when the first storm comes. This house is your home. You are going to live there the rest of your life. So you will want to make sure you don't build it poorly and with unstable materials. You want this house to be strong. You want it to be filled with peace, joy, love and hope. You want to be proud of your home. You want to know that it is solid through and through.

In essence, this is a metaphor for your life. You are going to be in your body for one lifetime. Do you build your character, which is the core of who you are, with unstable materials or with solid materials? Solid materials are discussed in this book. The choice is yours – what's it going to be? Are you worth it? Is your life worth it? My answer is that yes it is!

I remember hearing Pam Stenzel, a nationally known speaker, give a talk about counseling young teenage girls and the wild responses she got from them. I hear the same responses when I speak to young people. "If I had known the consequences. If someone had told me, I would have made different choices in life." You will find value in this book, if you allow it to expand the vision for your life, so you can make choices that develop character.

I am a little further down the road of life than you are. Imagine that I am a scout sent up the road ahead of you to check things out and give you a report. You can take my report and do what you want. If you ignore what I tell you, it could hurt you. Remember, wisdom only has value if you give it value. If you put it on the shelf in your mind, it will only sit there, be lifeless and collect dust. But if you apply it to your life, it will have effects on your destiny.

Making "BETTER" choices in life starts with asking better questions.
- "Is this the right thing to do?"
- "Will this hurt me or anyone else?"
- "Will this have a positive or negative effect?"

Great wisdom comes from the counsel of others. It's taking the time to ask someone about the choices laid before you. Ask your peers, but also make sure you ask a trusted adult. Make sure you ask someone who is willing to give you the best advice regardless of how you feel or whether you will get mad at him. This is your life we are talking about. Take the time to think about your choices. Start small. The quality of your life is composed of your daily choices. Big or small - all your choices count. You have a power. Use it wisely.

Daily Challenge:
1. What can you do to make better choices? Make a list for yourself.
2. Are there choices that you regret making? Why? What could you have done differently?

3.   Do you know someone you can talk to about your life choices? Who?

4.   Define some positive choices you can make for your life.

Day 3

CHARACTER STARTS WITH PERSONAL RESPONSIBILITY

Sam Glenn

"Soar with the strength of your own wings."

BAM! They told us not to go out on the road because it was busy and we could get hit by a car. We didn't listen. My brother Ben and I were on an adventure with our brand new ten speed bikes. We wanted to travel on them, so we decided to take the busy road and hope for the best. If we were careful enough, nobody would know and nobody would get hurt. I was wrong. I lay on the side of the road in a cornfield cut and bloody. I could see my bike had been totaled. I looked over and saw my brother Ben also cut up and laying about twenty feet away from me. His bike too was no more.

I asked Ben, "What happened? Where is the car that hit us?"

"What car? There is no car. Why did you stop?" Ben responded.

Then it occurred to me. I pulled over on the side of the road to scratch my leg and whammo! Ben hit me from behind. He was not watching where he was going. As we walked home carrying our brand new bikes that now looked like pretzels, we fought over whose fault it was. Ben kept saying it was my fault for stopping. I would argue back. "How can it be my fault? You weren't watching what was in front of you!"

I thought it was pretty obvious whose fault it was and that Ben did not want to get in trouble. When we got home, we had to deal with the music of Mom and Dad. Ben and I blamed each other. We went back and forth and our stories kept changing. The judges, Mom and Dad, came back with the verdict. It was both our fault. We chose to disobey Mom and Dad by going out on the busy road. None of this would have happened had we honored them. Neither of us wanted to claim ownership to this.

When I think of this time in my life, I think of the words "personal responsibility." We are responsible for our lives. I can't tell you how many times people come up to me complaining about this and that. What they are really doing is blaming someone or something for their problems or lack of success.

There are many people in this world who lack character. This is true of the world we live in, so watch out! When they disagree with you or get into a difficult situation, some of them will want to hurt you, get revenge, speak poorly of you to others and do more bad than good in the end. Why? Well, number one – lack of character. Number two, they don't know what personal responsibility is. Their beliefs about responsibility are jaded by untruths and compromise.

People of character accept personal responsibility for their lives, challenges, where they are at, where they are going, and the actions and words they use. People of character know that even sometimes they have to claim ownership to something that wasn't even their fault. Being responsible is being a giant when it comes to having a solid character. Think about it, if the archer missed the target, who and what is he going to blame? You are the archer for your life. You have nobody to blame but yourself if you are not living right and doing right, if you aren't hitting your mark. Nobody owes you a single thing - not the world, the guy next door, your parents, nobody! You were born with your own set of wings specifically designed for the purpose of soaring. If you are not using your own wings, there is no one else to blame! You have to take responsibility for your life because if you don't, who will?

We all face challenges that knock us down, but the question is and will always be: what are you going to do about it? Are you going to stay down and blame the world or get up, grow up, and move on? When you stop blaming others and making excuses as to why you are living the life that you are, you will gain a new and refreshing perspective on life. Take a deep breath. Let go of past resentments, hate, guilt, pain, or whatever feeling is hindering your best. Step to the edge of life and spread your wings.

Daily Challenge:

1. Do you point the finger at others more than yourself?

2. What does responsibility mean to you?

3. Why do you feel personal responsibility is important?

Day 4

LIVING A LIFE WITHOUT FINE PRINT

Mark Eiken

Saturday morning the paper came and there it was – the ad I had been waiting for. I was ready to purchase a VCR and there was one on sale for $99. By 10:00 o'clock in the morning I was at the store waiting for the doors to open. At 10:01 I was searching for the $99 VCR that was nowhere to be found. I asked the store clerk and showed him the ad. He said they did not have any more $99 VCR's although they did have some $150 ones. I showed him the picture of the VCR I wanted and said I got the ad this morning. They just opened and couldn't have sold their entire stock already. He then directed me to the "fine print" at the bottom of the ad. *"This product has limited quantities and may not be available in all locations."* What? Sometimes I hate fine print.

Have you ever had an experience like that? A situation looks a certain way, and then you read the fine print.

ONE BILLION FREE CELL MINUTES A MONTH!
Must be used between 3:30AM and 3:33AM on days beginning with the letter "M".
Only available on rate plans
$4,999.00 a month or more.

Do you know what I mean? Why does there have to be fine print? Why can't we just mean what we say and say what we mean?

Do you live your life with or without the "*fine print?*" Does your "yes" mean "yes" and your "no" mean "no"? Do you have to qualify your yeses and noes? For example, a very prominent political leader was involved in a sexual scandal a couple of years ago. He was asked a seemingly black and white question. "Did you have sexual relations with that woman?" He said, "No I did not have sexual relations with that woman...*according to my definition of sexual relations.*"

Character does not need to qualify its statements. Sometimes it means that we suffer consequences. Sometimes it brings conflict. Sometimes it is not popular. Always it reflects who you are and speaks volumes regarding your character.

If your mom asks if you studied for the test tomorrow and you say, "Yes...*for five minutes.*" That may get you out of studying more and out of the house for a while but it won't truthfully answer the question you were being asked and it won't pass the test for you. It will, however, *speak loud and clear about your character.*

You see, "fine print" is deceptive because it isn't made known unless it is sought out. Back to the previous example: Mom asks if you studied, you say "yes." Only if she asks, "For how long?" will the whole truth be made known. We know deep inside that saying yes to the question isn't totally honest, and partially honest doesn't count. Character doesn't need fine print.

Daily Challenge:

1. How does it make you feel when people are not totally upfront with you or you have to dig for the truth?

2. List a couple of ways that you have used "fine print." You may find you need to speak to some people to set the record straight.

3. Make a commitment today to eliminate "fine print" from your life. Say, "Even if it is tough, even if it means extra work or I have to sacrifice a night out, I will let my "yes" and my "no" stand alone. *NO FINE PRINT!*

SECTION TWO

Character and You

Day 5

THE WORTH OF A LIFE

Sam Glenn

*"Once you realize the awesome reason that you are here,
life can never be the same!" – Ron Hutchcraft*

*"We become responsible for the thoughts we hold in
our brain and the ones we add to it."*

Kirk looked like an alien. He had huge thick glasses that magnified the size of his eyes. His hair resembled that of Marge on *The Simpsons*. His voice was high pitched, like life would not let him out of puberty prison. The retainer was the cherry on top. Imagine sticking an entire orange in your mouth and how big your mouth would look. That was Kirk. Plus, it made him drool. To say the least, he looked funny. I thought it was awesome! He was my special friend.

Back in junior high he looked different. He was going through changes, but what always upset me were those who made fun of him. I always told Kirk to fight back, but that wasn't his solution to this challenge. He once shared with me that it did not matter. It didn't matter what anybody said. He had a choice to believe it or not and he chose to never believe the negative things people spoke about him.

You and I have the same choice. It's not an easy one, but a choice we do have. Sure, we desire to be accepted and feel valued, but first we must accept ourselves and value ourselves. If we are always trying to please others, we lose our true selves. Instead of living our lives the way we should, we are living it the way others would have us.

17

Our self-worth is not who we know, what we own, what we drive or achieve. Our self-worth is rooted in the truth that each of us was born with–value and worth. You don't have to attain things or impress others to gain self-worth. You already have it. You don't have to look a certain way or be a certain way. Just believe you have self-worth.

Truth also be known, people will make fun of you and put you down. That seems to just be a part of life. You are not going to please everyone. But you have a choice in what you believe about what others say about you. If you know the truth, then it doesn't matter what anybody says. The truth will stand longer than a lie. You may not be able to control what others think of you, but you can control what you think about yourself. Your self-image is how you see yourself. If you feel bad about you, that's your choice. If you feel good, that too is your choice.

Nobody can change who you are or how you feel without your permission.

You are a person of worth and value! That should be your truth. Know it, live it and walk in it! Say it out loud, "I am a person of worth and value! This is the truth!" Say it again! Believe it!

Daily Challenge:

1. Do you worry about what others say or think of you?

2. Do you make choices based upon what others might think of you?

3. Do you compromise your true self to be accepted or to fit in?

4. What makes you feel worthless?

5. What makes you feel valued?

6. List some of the positive qualities that you like about yourself.

Day 6

A NEW LANGUAGE

Sam Glenn

There is a proverb that says, "As a man thinks, so he is."

"You become what you think about all day long."

It is said that a majority of our self-talk is negative. Almost eighty percent! We believe what we hear. We live what we believe. Therefore, the results in our lives reflect what is in our minds and what we speak to ourselves.

Recently, a young girl came up to me and started to share bits and pieces about her life. She felt like her life was getting better, but as she talked with me, she kept saying negative things about herself. Each time she said something negative about herself, I jumped in and joyfully said something positive about her. She was not understanding me, or hearing me. The voice in her mind was louder. She kept following me around and talking and talking, which I did not mind. An adult who knew her told me that it was a very nice gesture on my part to encourage her. I didn't think anything of it - that's what I do.

As this girl followed me, she kept talking and ripping on herself and how bad life was. Something in me snapped. I couldn't listen to it any more. I looked at her and said, "STOP!" Her eyes got huge! I looked her in the eyes and said, "Please stop tearing yourself down. You have been given this gift of life and you're selling yourself short."

I informed her that she needed to develop a new language. Her internal self-talk was destroying her and tearing her down. It was making her feel bad about herself, others and life. I explained to her that each day she has to practice with new words. You have to turn the negatives into positives, and then repeat them to yourself over and over. As a result you will think differently, believe differently, live differently, and act differently. It's very powerful!

Daily Challenge:

1. Do you need to change some words that you speak to yourself?

2. What negative phrases can you replace with positive ones?

3. The key is to practice. You must apply it immediately. Make a conscious effort to stop negative self-talk and replace it with positive phrases.

The words you speak to yourself over and over will form into a habit and become part of your character. Habit is something formed doing the same thing over and over and over and over and over again.

Day 7

HAVE A GOOD SENSE OF HUMOR

Sam Glenn

"Learn to laugh at yourself!"

I love to laugh. I look in the mirror and laugh. You try it! Laughter has power for living life to the fullest. I have never felt as good as when I do when I am laughing or having a good sense of humor about something. It makes us feel good, look good and releases endorphins into the body, which are natural pain killers and gives us a natural high. In the workplace, in the home, and in life having the joy of humor is a must! Without a sense of humor, it's like driving a car on a bumpy road without shocks!

Humor is like a muscle. The more you use it, the more it develops and the easier it is to laugh. It first starts by learning to laugh at yourself in a healthy way. In fact the best humor will be the things you do and say. You have to practice using your humor muscle. Learn to laugh at the pure and positive things, not the sick and tasteless. Never laugh at the expense of others. That's negative and wrong. Laugh at the good stuff around you. Fake it at first if you have to, but soon enough it will transform into real laughter. Laughter can change your day, your attitude, and your life!

Let me share a story with you where having a good sense of humor played a huge role. I was flying into Tampa, Florida to speak for a large group. I was coming off a four-hour flight. It was not a very comfortable flight. So when I got off, I really did not feel like being there. I was tired, hungry, and a bit ornery. I put on a nice smile for the group that was picking me up and away we all proceeded down to the luggage carousel to retrieve my luggage. When we got down there, we heard all these people laughing. Now whenever there is laughter, I have to see what it is about. I looked as all these people where pointing to some luggage on the carousel that did not look right. I looked and saw that some guy's poor luggage had ripped in half and the airlines taped it up with clear tape, but when they taped it up, they taped his underwear to the outside of the case. It looked so funny. I began laughing as everybody was laughing. As I was laughing and tears were steaming down my face, the funny luggage with the undies on the outside got closer, it began to look very familiar. As it passed me, shock and reality set in, and I responded to my host, "That is mine!"

He said, "No way! Are you kidding? Are you going to get it?"

"No way, not with all these people watching and laughing! What do I look like a side show?"

To say the least, I was confused and in shock. My luggage passed me by over six times. I couldn't believe it. Nobody was leaving! They wanted to see who owned the funny luggage with the underwear packed on the outside. **I was now faced with a choice, as we all are in life's situations like this.** I could have screamed, complained and told people to shut up. It was a choice I had, but I saw the joy my situation was creating. So, with a smile, I reached down and grabbed the luggage. The crowd began to point, clap and cheer. It put a huge smile on my face. It also changed my attitude. I wasn't as grumpy. I didn't feel as bad. In fact, I felt pretty good! That's the power of humor.

Daily Challenge:
1. Is there something from your past that wasn't funny at the time, but could be funny now?

Day 8

I WANNA BE LIKE ....
ME!

Jason Palmisano

At least one night a week, I make a huge bowl of popcorn and watch a Disney movie with my kids (Haley - 4, Michael - 3, Joshua - 1½ and Samuel 2 weeks). It's one of our little traditions. We have about every Disney movie imaginable. My kids take turns picking the movie, but every now and then they get in a rut. What I mean is they pick the same movie over and over and over again. Their current rut is "Toy Story 2". We've watched it to infinity and beyond! Their last rut was Walt Disney's "Jungle Book."

The story is about a boy named Mowgli. As an infant he had been left behind in the jungle and was raised by a pack of wolves. By the time he is ten, he hunts, howls and eats like a wolf. Then one day, Shere Khan, the tiger comes to the jungle and is a threat to Mowgli's life. In an attempt to save the boy, the animals decide to return Mawgli to his own people. On his way to the human village, Mowgli meets Baloo the bear. Baloo takes Mowgli under his wing and teaches him all about the "bear" necessities of life. As a result, Mowgli begins to act as a bear. He does the same thing with elephants and then with swinging King Louie and the chimpanzees. Mowgli goes from group to group to group trying to fit in by being something he isn't. I remember in college, I experienced the "Mowgli" syndrome first-hand!

After high school, I signed a full scholarship to play wide receiver for the University of North Carolina Tar Heels. Our quarterback was Mark. He was a star athlete, a senior, good looking, engaged to be married and had an almost perfect grade point average. Everybody loved Mark. As a young freshman on campus, Mark was my role model and my hero. I thought if I could just be like Mark, then everyone would like me too. So I hung around Mark and studied him. After a while, I started to imitate him. Following his example wasn't a bad thing, I just took things too far. As perfect as he was, Mark did have one flaw - a speech impediment that caused him to stu-stu-stutter. I wanted to be like him so much that I even started to imitate his stutter. Talk about crazy! Can you imagine how foolish I must have sounded to those who already knew my speech to be fine? Needless to say, trying to be like Mark did not last long. I finally realized that I would never be just like him and that I was better off working on being me. He had some great qualities that I didn't, but the reverse was also true.

There is only one you. Be you the best you can. Resist the temptation to be a cheap imitation of someone else. **You are unique, original and awesome**. A strong character is developed through recognizing who you are, the good and the bad, and making the best of it. **Live out your life as YOU, with courage and honesty**. Success, fulfillment and contentment will be right there too.

Daily Challenge:
1. Is there someone you have tried to be like?
2. What are some unique qualities you possess?

SECTION THREE

Character and Courage

Day 9

THE COURAGE TO FACE YOUR FEARS

Sam Glenn

"Courage is getting the chicken out of you."

"Fear has no power other than what you give it."

When I was a little Sammy living in Minnesota, I remember I hated walking home from the bus stop. It was about two blocks and there was this one house that had the ugliest, meanest dog that would chase me. Everyday I feared that walk home. I would hope and pray the dog would not be outside. If he were, he would chase me and bark up a storm. I was afraid that thing was going to shred me to bits.

One day, as I slowly walked the edge of the yard where this creature lived, I looked over some bushes, saw nothing, and kept walking. Then, it happened. "AHHHHHHHH!" Out of nowhere came my worst fear. He was barking and had a look in his eyes that he was on a mission to eat a little boy. I got so scared that I ran into someone else's house. I began to cry and screamed at the dog to go away. When the people who owned the house saw me, they came to help and pointed out that the dog was old and had no teeth. He only wanted to play with me. I was afraid for nothing. I gave something power over my life that could not really hurt me.

I think many of us do that in areas of our life. Maybe we fail at something and we are fearful to try again. Perhaps somebody says something and we are fearful of what others might say. Fear should not have control over you.

It's hard to live life to the fullest if you are afraid all the time - afraid to try, do, go and become. You were put here for a reason, don't let your fears keep you from living life to the fullest.

Daily Challenge:

1. What fear is keeping you from trying something you have always wanted to try?

2. List some fears that you think may be keeping your from your best.

3. What actions can you take to overcome some of your fears?

4. Who can you talk to about this?

Day 10

COURAGE, CONVICTION AND CHARACTER

Mark Eiken

"Courage is not simply one of the virtues, but the form of every virtue at its testing point." ~ C. S. Lewis

"The difference between a hero and a coward is one step sideways." ~ Gene Hackman

"Courage is being scared to death but saddling up anyway." ~ John Wayne

A person of unshakable character will undoubtedly come across situations that require courageous decisions. In fact, the stronger your character, the more often it will be tested. I will go as far as to say that how your character stands in adversity, is the best measuring stick for your character. In other words, when your convictions are challenged, how you respond reflects the strength of your character.

To help you stand firm when your convictions are challenged, here are a couple of very important questions you need to ask yourself. The first is, where is "the line in the sand?" For example, when it comes to sex, where is your line in the sand? Have you ever even thought about it? Will I hold hands? Will I kiss? Will I go "all the way?" What are the consequences of each? As a person of character, you will want to make a decision based upon the long-term benefits or consequences. I know that many young people now realize the importance of sexual purity and they are making a very clear "line in the sand." They have chosen abstinence until marriage. More and more students are realizing that the ultimate in sexuality is experienced in a loving, committed marriage, so they have made the decision to wait. This is a line that will be challenged often. That is why courage is so important in building an unshakable character.

"The ultimate measure of a man is not where he stands in moments of comfort and convenience, but where he stands at times of challenge and controversy,"
~ Martin Luther King, Jr.

The best way I've learned to be able to stand courageously when my convictions are challenged is I put myself in the position *before* I get there. I think of a conviction and a situation in which it could be challenged. Then I plan out my response. For example, I have a conviction that I do not want to drink alcohol. I play out a scenario in my mind of how that could be challenged. Maybe I'm out with the girl I've always dreamed about dating and we stop by a friend's house. We are having a great time. Then out comes the beer. My girl starts drinking and encourages me to have a few also. I have a choice. If I say no, my dream date may be over. If I say all right, my character is shaken and the next day I'll be wishing that my "dream" date were really a dream because I sacrificed a part of my character. So in advance of that happening, I plan out my response. This way I eliminate, as much as possible, the desires and influences of the moment.

It takes great courage to stand
for your convictions;
it is much easier to stand when you
are certain what they are.

Daily Challenge:

1. Define your convictions. Where do you draw your "lines in the sand?" Look at relationships: dating, respecting parents, friendships, teachers. Look at behavior: actions that are questionable and activities that may or may not be beneficial. Look at your academics. Look at your spiritual life. Where do you stand in all these areas?

Day 11

THE MADMAN, THE LAW

Rolfe Carawan

He was the most hated and vilified congressman of his time—a stubborn, ill-humored old man who delighted in agitating his peers. During his time in office, Monday was the official petition day in the House of Representatives. On that day, any member of the House could introduce petitions to the membership for consideration. And every Monday morning, his fellow congressmen entered the chamber with a feeling of great dread. If they spotted the shiny bald head of this rookie legislator in seat 203 of the House they knew they were in for a very long day. It seemed he always came in with the same set jaw, the same determined look. And when he stood to speak, it was always about the same thing: "that abominable law" as he put it. At one point, it was reported that he had introduced 900 petitions against it—in one day! One of his fellow congressmen called him a "mischievous, bad old man" and some newspapers dubbed him the "madman of Massachusetts."

Who was this divisive troublemaker? Who was this rabble-rouser who dared to speak against a law that had been legitimized by every government since 1787? He was John Quincy Adams. His courageous battle against slavery provoked some of the most explosive showdowns and outrageous maneuvers in congressional history. His stand was all the more noteworthy because he didn't have to take it at all.

His reputation and his place in history were already secured. As the sixth President of the United States, he was entitled to retire to a life of reflective ease. But when his neighbors approached him in 1830 to run as their congressman after his loss to Andrew Jackson in the presidential race, he accepted the honor and was handily elected. And so he arrived back in Washington, D.C., as a 63-year-old freshman congressman, beginning perhaps the greatest struggle of his political life.

As early as 1820, Adams had been engaged in the growing controversy over slavery. He had publicly spoken against it on moral grounds in debates with John C. Calhoun, all the while hoping a more articulate spokesman would take up the cause. But in the House of Representatives in 1830, there was a no more articulate spokesman to be found than Adams was himself; and he took his place with a tremendous sense of duty and purpose.

By 1836, some Southern Congressmen had had enough. Voting 117 to 68, they passed a gag rule that tabled all petitions relating to slavery, allowing no discussion whatsoever, much less referral to committee for action. For the next eight years, continuing gag rules were adopted. And during those eight years, Adams continued to present his petitions, using every bit of expertise and cunning his forty years in politics had given him. He managed to get the substance of each petition itself, artfully asking if a petition stating "such and such" would be against "the rule." His daily battle to repeal the gag rules infuriated his opponents as much as his stand against slavery. He could never rise to his feet to speak without enduring a jarring round of ridicule, repeated motions of censure and loud calls for his expulsion. But his courage never flagged. He remained a constant irritant to the status quo, a constant prod to the slow of conscience, a constant reminder of the immorality and illogic of men owning men, a constant voice for those he represented.

Finally, in 1844, the twenty-first gag rule was repealed. Adams had won the right to continue to petition against slavery. By that time, even his enemies acknowledged his courage and integrity. They called him "Old Man Eloquent." He died in 1846 after collapsing at his desk in the House, never having seen the abolition of the law he so despised.

While he accomplished many other great things in his career, John Quincy Adams' prolonged battle in Congress to abolish slavery has marked him perhaps even more than his presidency as a man of unflagging moral courage. He dared to speak out when it was neither comfortable nor safe to do so. He dared to speak out when his personal reputation and safety were threatened. And he continued to speak out when there seemed to be no hope that he would ever be heard. That is the essence of courage—doing what is right simply because it is right to do so.

Daily Challenge:

1. Is there something you are willing to take a stand for? If so what? Why?

2. Think about times when your convictions were challenged. What was your response?

3. Visualize yourself making courageous decisions that build character. Replaying your previous and past reactions will also show you areas that you have not defined your boundaries and convictions for.

SECTION FOUR

Character and Respect

Day 12

LIVE A LIFE OF HONOR
Jeff Canfield

*"Honor is showing value and respect
towards people, places and things."*

I became a police officer on October 5, 1987. My first day on the job the officer conducting the orientation handed me a gun and a badge. I could hardly believe it! *It's wonderful when a dream becomes a reality*!

I had no idea at the time that God was going to use my law enforcement experience to help prepare me for a future ministry. I would also find out that my idealistic view of law enforcement, and the respect that I had for those in the profession, was not shared by as large a segment of the population as I had thought.

After I had been an officer for several years, someone asked me what were the most shocking things in law enforcement. They might have expected an answer like, "*the bloody crime scenes*," or "*the dangerous situations*." My answer might have surprised them. **What was most shocking to me was the utter disrespect for the police**.

However, I do have to say I worked the night shift seven out of eight years I was in law enforcement. This means I dealt with the part of society that normal, average, everyday citizens don't see unless their house is being burglarized. I understand that these people have an obvious dislike for the police. Disrespect from criminals is to be expected.

What amazed me was the lack of respect from the *non-criminals*. I'm referring to the other kids on the block who, for the most part, are not interested getting in trouble. The type of kids who stand back and watch as the infamous players in their neighborhood are routinely chased by the police. They develop a deep dislike for the police, seeing them as an enemy.

I'll never forget how shocked I was having a sixteen-year-old stand face to face with me and cuss me up one side and down the other. Or, on another occasion, a young man jumped out of a crowd, into the middle of the street in front of one of our squad cars on patrol. Next, he pulled down his pants and exposed himself while shouting profanities, then ran off the street disappearing into the crowd.

Our outward displays of honor and respect come from beliefs that are formed within us. Our five physical senses help form many of our beliefs as we grow from childhood to young adults. What we see modeled in front of us, what we hear being taught to us, and the love and discipline that we feel.

Despite the surroundings in which we are raised, which many times are beyond our control, we must make a concerted effort to treat all people with respect and honor. The world has a saying that what ever goes around comes around. If we want others to respect us, then we must show respect for others. True success in this life will only come by living a life of honor. Solomon said, "Do you see a man who excels in his work? He will stand before kings, and not before unknown men." Keep in mind, criminals only become famous when they are caught and tried. **On the other hand, we build timeless memorials to those who have lived honorable lives**.

Treating others with respect must become a lifestyle. *Be different!* Be a person who shows honor and respect to others despite their actions toward you. Even if you don't see results right away, *respect will come back around*. **Live a life of honor and you will excel!** You will stand before important men and women because you have laid a foundation of honor in your life, and in turn you will be honored.

Daily Challenge:
1. What does respect mean to you?
2. What are some ways to demonstrate respect to others?
3. How should you respond if friends are being disrespectful?

Day 13

HONORING OUR PARENTS

Jeff Canfield

"Honoring parents is a commandment, not a suggestion."

I was dispatched to a home one night where a single mother was having problems with her teenage son. The teenager was passed out on the bathroom floor with his face in a puddle of vomit.

He had been out drinking all evening with friends. I picked him up and laid him on his bed. He came to for just a moment and looked right at his mother. His mother said, "Why are you doing this to me?"

I was amazed at what came out of this drunken teenager's mouth. He said, "Mom, *you don't discipline me enough.* Other kids' parents care where they're at and who they're with, *you just don't care.*" I felt as if a standing ovation was in order for this drunken teenager. How can anyone ignore a cry for help like that?

Ideally it's best to have a mother and father both at home raising the children with each sharing in the responsibilities, and using the gifts and abilities that have been instilled in them to raise their children. However, *we don't live in an ideal society.* In many homes today, kids are an innocent party of divorce and are being raised by a single parent, or a parent hurt by a spouse who was abusive or unfaithful. Now the parent is left dealing with all the parental responsibilities alone. Parents in this situation may be dealing with bitterness and hatred toward an ex-spouse while experiencing feelings of condemnation, wondering if they themselves are to blame.

On top of that, they may have children who have been hurt by witnessing mom or dad walk out on the family. The child may also be dealing with feelings of guilt and even hatred toward the delinquent parent, which in turn makes it very difficult for the child to honor their mother and father.

However, submission to those in authority over us (*parents, teachers, employers*) **is an act of our will.** Submitting doesn't always mean we're in complete agreement, or that those in authority over us have to be perfect first. Remember this, the people that we have to show honor and respect toward are a lot like us - *they're not perfect either.* Nevertheless, in order to show honor and respect to those in authority over us *we must continually show a willingness to comply with rules and instructions.*

Some might say, "*Yeah, but you don't know how my parents have hurt me, and caused so much pain in my life!*" Maybe I've never walked in your shoes, but ask yourself this: "Does a person have to walk in someone else's shoes in order to distinguish right from wrong?"

I would challenge you not to allow the bad that's happened in your life to determine your destiny. Bad roots develop into bad trees. **You control your destiny!** And, whether you realize it or not the outcome, *and the amount of success you have*, will be determined by the quality of honor and respect you show to others. *Live a life of honor - no matter what the cost!*

Daily Challenge:

1. What does it mean to honor your parents?
2. Define honor?
4. Should you disrespect your parents in any way and for any reason?
5. If your parents treat you poorly or unfairly, is it honorable to do the same back to them?
6. What are ways that you personally can be honorable towards your mom or dad?

Character and Anger

Day 14

ANGER: UNDER CONTROL OR NOT?

Sam Glenn

"Anger is like fire. When it's in the fireplace it's controlled, but when it's in the middle of the house, it's out of control."

If there is one character element many people struggle with, it's maintaining self-control when they're angry. We live in a world of road rage and fast food. When things don't go our way, it's easy to get angry. How should we respond when we get angry?

First let's identify anger. Anger can come from many things, such as feeling betrayed, being treated badly, getting ripped off, being cheated, or any number of other causes. When faced with a difficult situation, it is easy to lack self-control, which can result in our anger getting out of control.

I was recently at the airport and my flight was delayed for almost three hours. To say the least, it was upsetting. But, there was nothing we could really do. The plane had mechanical problems. Well, this one fellow walks up to the counter and begins to let the ticket agent have it. He is screaming his head off, "I want satisfaction! I want your name! You're all fired! Your airline this! Your airline that!" The man put on a poor display of character. His anger was out of control. Anyone watching could see that. Still there was nothing the agent could do. The plane needed to be fixed and it would be three hours no matter how much he ranted and raved. Did this man solve anything? No. Did he make himself or anyone else feel better? No. Did he handle his anger in the right way? No.

I remember hearing a story about a professional football player who, if his team lost, would go home and literally saw his car in half with a chain saw. Another time, when I was in college, I saw a basketball player put his fist through a glass window because he was mad at his girlfriend. Can you think of an instance where you saw someone angry and totally out of control? Have you ever let your anger get out of control?

Anger is something you must face head-on, but you must know how to face it and deal with it. No one ever benefits from anger that is out of control. By learning to use self-control with anger, you will benefit personally, in your relationships with family and friends, at school, and in your professional life. You will get better results and find more workable solutions. My hope is that you challenge yourself to learn how to handle anger.

Daily Challenge:

1. What do you think are some additional benefits to managing your emotions when you are angry?

2. What do you think are some negative things that could happen if your anger gets out of control?

Day 15

PRACTICE SELF-CONTROL

Sam Glenn

Practice makes improvement! Progress comes before perfection!

Remember, whatever you do over and over and over will become a habit. If you do good things repeatedly, they will develop and strengthen your character. Self-control can be applied to many areas of our lives, but here we will focus on self-control when applied to anger.

Why do people flip out so easily and lose control of their anger? Why does one person have self-control and another behaves like the devil? Much of it has to do with the influence in our lives. We see how our favorite actors respond to anger in the media, we watch mom and dad, and we observe what our friends do in these situations. These all influence our responses. I want to create a new awareness for you in responding to the emotion of anger.

The vital questions you need to ask yourself are: "Do my responses hurt or harm others? Do my responses help the situation or make it worse? Do I seek revenge or do I seek understanding? Do I scream at others, use foul language or turn to destructive behavior such as smoking, drinking or drugs?

The truth is that challenges and difficulties are part of life. You cannot avoid them. You may have one or one hundred challenges in a day. Either way, day-to-day challenges require the right response. Practicing the right responses will help you deal with them better and faster.

Daily Challenge:

    1. What ways have you responded in the past when angry?

    2. Do your responses make the situation better or worse?

    3. Who do you think has had the biggest influence on you as far as your responses when you are angry?

    4. What would you change about your usual responses when you get angry?

Day 16

RESPONSES TO ANGER

Sam Glenn

*"Are you going to be a part of the problem,
or a part of the solution?"*

Every challenge requires a response. Every challenge has the potential to make you grow or knock you down. If you allow challenges to knock you down, you get angry. Sometimes we get so mad that we respond immediately without thinking it through. Sometimes we lose control when we let anger build over time and then we explode. If you let anger sit inside you, it will rot you out. Anger gives life to hate, resentment, and actions that are destructive.

Sometimes situations arise that are beyond our control. In these situations, the only control we do have is in how we respond. For example, how would you respond if someone breaks into your home and steals everything, scratches your new car, and kicks your dog? What if your mom and dad tell you "No!" to something you really wanted? Perhaps your significant other leaves you. Things like these would really make me mad, but I know that throwing a tantrum will not help the situation. Cussing someone out will not help. Being violent will not help. So the question is, how can we respond to demonstrate a solid character?

HOW CAN YOU RESPOND IN A WAY THAT WILL BRING OUT THE "BETTER" IN YOU AND NOT THE "WORSE"?

Do:

- Get around people who can help you deal with the situation.
- Take the time to grieve and be angry, write down how you feel.
- Seek to understand the situation.
- Seek to forgive.
- Exercise, take a walk, or run.
- Call someone for advice.

Don't:

- Make major decisions or do anything drastic.
- Seek revenge.
- Egg someone's home.
- Rebel.
- Hurt yourself or anyone else.
- Start a fight.
- Cuss or throw a temper tantrum.

**Remember: Violence is not the answer.
Destructive behavior never works.**

Nobody ever wins with destructive intentions.

Daily Challenge:
1. List 5 ways you will choose to respond the next time you get angry? (These 5 ways must bring out your "better" and not your "worse.")

Day 17

WIPE THE POOP OFF YOUR FACE

Bobby Petrocelli

"Attitude is everything!" – Keith Harrell

A young man was walking down the beach, then suddenly out of nowhere wham! A seagull poops right in his face. Instead of wiping off the poop, he leaves it there. Can you believe it? He became so angry at the seagull. He reasoned within himself and said, "That seagull did this to me and he is going to have to come back and get this poop off of me!" When he returns to his friends they are all repulsed. "What is that smell? Stay away from us", they shouted. Then they all ran away from him. He became even angrier with the seagull, "Look what you've done to me," the man cried. "You come back here right now and get this off of me!"

He goes over to his girlfriend's house to watch some television. She immediately kicks him out of the house and demands that he washes his face. He lies on the steps of her house feeling rejected and lonely, contemplating how the seagull was ruining his life. His friends had run away and now his girlfriend doesn't want anything to do with him. All he could think was, "It's not my fault!"

When he goes to work the next day, people quickly go to the other side of the room to avoid him. The odor has become unbearable. The man had stopped bathing, because if he bathed he might remove the poop from his face, then the seagull would have gotten by with his unfair treatment of him.

Finally, his boss called him in and said, "None of your clients want to do business with you. None of your co-workers can stand to be in the same room with you. Either you wash that poop off your face or you are fired!" The man's response was, "How unfair! Why are you persecuting me? I didn't do anything wrong. I didn't put this on my face. I shouldn't have to be the one to wash it off."

This is a silly story, yet people go through life with unforgiveness everyday. Millions of people go through pain everyday, feeling that someone else should come and fix the pain they inflicted. The truth is, it will never happen. If you want to be free from the past, quit living for the past.

Daily Challenge:
1. Are you holding a grudge toward anyone? What ways can you begin to start forgiving them?

Forgiving them is like wiping the poop off your face. Be in charge of your destiny. Choose to forgive. Forgiving is learning from the past NOT running from the past.

Day 18

FORGIVING THE IMPOSSIBLE

Gina Waegele

"Forgiveness equals freedom."

My sister Christine had a smile that would light up the room. When she laughed, everyone around her would want to laugh. She brought joy to the people around her. While we were growing up, my sister always talked about staying at home with her children. Christine got married, had three children and then got divorced. Even though her first marriage didn't work out, her dream finally came true. Another man came along and promised to take care of her and her three children. Shortly into her new marriage, Christine was able to quit her job and stay home with her children like she always wanted. A week later, this same man, who promised her the world, took his bare hands and strangled her to death while her children were at home.

For the four years following my sister's death, I carried hate and bitterness in my heart for the man who chose to end my sister's life. I became bitter at the world. In my everyday life, I noticed that I would become angry and impatient about very small things that didn't go my way.

I became angry at other people for things I shouldn't have been upset about, but found that I was still angry with the murderer of my sister. My life hit an all time low. I got involved in unhealthy relationships and destructive behavior. I would walk around during the day, pretending I was fine and then out of the blue, I would get angry. At night when I would come home from work or school, I would get depressed. Rarely was there a night that I didn't cry myself to sleep. I wanted to control my anger and not be so depressed, so I went to a counselor. Right away, she pre-scribed me depression pills. As I held the bottle in my hand that night, I felt God's presence and Him saying, "Gina, you don't need this, you need Me." I listened and obeyed. Immediately my life was transformed.

I knew that I could not continue on with my life unless I forgave the murderer of my sister. It didn't mean I had to tell him. It wasn't as if he ever asked for my forgiveness. For all I know, he may not be truly sorry. Forgiving him did not mean that he shouldn't suffer the consequences of what he did. Forgiving him meant that he would no longer have control in my life. As long as I stayed bitter and harbored hate in my life, the longer he would have control over my actions and my attitude.

No matter how great or small a person's offense is toward you, it only hurts yourself to hate and be bitter. As long as you stay angry, the offender has control in your life. This offender is keeping you from experiencing joy. Joy is when you are able to see past current circumstances and not let them bring you down. Forgive those who have offended you. It doesn't take away the circumstances, but it will make you feel a lot better. I will always miss my sister, but I know that she would want me to be experiencing the joy I have now rather than the hate I had in the past.

Daily Challenge:
1. Do you need to forgive someone?
2. What is keeping you from forgiveness?
3. Ask yourself "How will I be different when I forgive?"

SECTION SIX

Character and Community

Day 19

CITIZENSHIP

Josh Shipp

"Treat the world as you wish the world to treat you."
— Bruce Anderson, Broadcaster, Durango, Colorado

"Youth are not the leader of tomorrow,
youth are the LEADERS OF TODAY!"
— Josh Shipp

How often do you see a report on the news of a young person doing something good? Very rarely, I'm sure. I know that is the case where I live. It seems like anytime I turn on the television, and a young person is on the news, it is for something related to drugs, alcohol, school violence, or some other crime. The TRUTH is that this is <u>not</u> a good representation of the youth of America. Most young people are involved, passionate about life and about making a difference.

<u>Do you want to change the stereotype</u>
<u>that some adults have of youth?</u>

GET INVOLVED!

Volunteer, mentor, tutor, or join student or community organizations. Don't ever think that you are too young to do something important. I started speaking professionally when I was 19 years old. I remember how hard it was at first being young and wanting to do something so huge. It seemed like all I heard was, "You're too young!" "You need to go to college first." "You need to have a family first!" "You can't do that!" The truth is that if you have a burning passion and desire in you to make a difference YOU CAN!

Don't procrastinate...REGULATE!
"If not now, then when?
If not you, then who?"

Don't sit around and say, "Oh someone else will help out. I don't need to." Use your gifts and talents to help your community. Think about what you have to give that would benefit the community and make it a better place for everyone. Large or small, everyone has something of value to give.

Here are some suggestions:
- Attend city meetings. Often at these meetings adults will sit around and talk about what is best for young people. Wouldn't it be cool if there were a young person there that could say what is best for youth?
- Volunteer at a local organization. This could also give you some awesome job experience and a behind the scenes look at what goes on at a business or organization. When I was younger I wanted to be a doctor. I spent about eight hours with a doctor in my community and I thought it was awful. But at least I didn't wait to find out after I was in medical school that I hated it! Sometimes finding out what you do want to do in life is about finding out what you *don't* want to do.
- Rent and watch the movie, "Pay it forward." Put this to practice in your own life.
- Mentor younger students. Help them with their homework; go get ice cream with them. Play tic-tac-toe with them! **WARNING**: I have found most sixth grade stu-

dents are unusually good at tic-tac-toe. You better have
your game face on!

- Citizenship can be displayed in very simple ways to.
Returning your shopping cart to the "shopping cart
lodge." Picking up a piece of trash you see somewhere.
Opening a door for a stranger. Mowing an elderly couple's yard. Or, just smile at a stranger.

**Unfortunately some adults have a negative opinion
about young people because of what they see on the
news. YOU CAN CHANGE THAT!**

Day 20

BE AVAILABLE!

Ben Glenn

*"Success is going from one failure to the next
without losing enthusiasm."
— Winston Churchill*

When I was a freshman in high school, I got voted to be
the guy to promote the school-wide food drive at lunch one
day. Nobody else wanted to do it, so I thought "Why not?"
Initially, I wasn't too keen on the whole thing, but I spent
some time preparing a little skit and speech and I hoped
that students would be inspired to bring in their parents'
canned goods.

The fateful day came and I was ready. I had decided that
this was my big chance to make a name for myself at the
school. I knew the babes weren't going to leave me alone
once they saw my skillful presentation. Needless to say, I

completely humiliated myself in front of the entire school - three times! After lunch, I found myself keeping a low profile in all my classes, I was convinced that the food-drive would generate exactly one can of non-perishable goods - mine! With failure looming, I was sure that I had made a huge mistake accepting the responsibility of being the spokesperson. At the end of the week, upon the final count of the food brought in for the drive, it was determined that that year's food drive was, by far, the most successful that the school had ever had. Was it a coincidence? Dumb luck? Perhaps.

I learned an important lesson from that experience: Sometimes, just being **available** to do the job can make a world of difference. Not only to others, but to yourself as well. Getting up in front of the whole school all those years ago, gave me my first taste for public speaking and though my rookie presentation was far from impressive, looking back I realize that my love for being "up front" was actually born right around that time. Now of course, public speaking is my life! And, hard to believe as it is, the first public school assembly I gave as a professional speaker was at, you guessed it – my old high school!

Being available is a vital character quality that doesn't get the attention it deserves. **Availability indicates a purposeful desire to help others and put them before our own needs and schedule.** Remember that when we help others by making ourselves available to them, their success will spill back into our lives.

Daily Challenge:
    1. Make a list of people who could use your help, but haven't been getting it.
    2. Now go and lend them a hand already!

3. Is there a group or organization that would benefit from your efforts in working with them? Check it out and get involved and volunteer.

Day 21

VALUING PEOPLE

Mark Eiken

"You can't make someone feel important if secretly inside you think he is a nobody"

The Queen of England often visits Ballmoral Castle. On one occasion when she was walking by herself, it started to rain. She rushed to the shelter of the nearest cottage. A lady came to the door and was really ticked off that someone would bother her at that time in the morning. She opened the door a few inches and barked, "What do you want?" The queen didn't introduce herself. She merely asked, "May I borrow an umbrella. "Just a minute," grumbled the woman. She slammed the door, was gone for a moment, and returned bringing the rattiest umbrella she could find, one with broken ribs and small holes. "Here." The Queen of England thanked her and went on her way with the ragged umbrella.

The next morning, the queen's full escort, dressed in full uniform, pulled up in front of the cottage. One of the escorts knocked on the door and returned the umbrella to the woman saying, "Madam, the Queen of England thanks you." As he walked away he heard her mutter, "If I'd only known, I'd have given her my best."

Have you ever been treated badly? Maybe you have asked someone for help and they didn't view your situation as importantly as you did, and they gave you second best effort. There are people who can make you feel like a king or a queen by the way they respond to you. There are also those who make you feel like a peasant – unimportant and unworthy. Nobody likes to feel unimportant. Some of the people I respect and admire most are also people who have an ability to add to my life by valuing me as a person.

The way you respond to people says a lot about your character. Part of character is the value you place upon people. The problem is that we often look at people from the perspective of, "What can they do for me?" or "How can I benefit from them?" If they can't help me, if they can't do something for me, if they can't make me look better, then they are unimportant in my life. Do our words or actions devalue our peers? Think about the people you do or don't hang out with at school. The person who sits alone in the lunchroom has value. The quarterback of the football team has value. You may be best friends with neither, but they both should be valued as fellow human beings.

A person of character values people and adds value to their lives. A person of unshakable character looks to build others up, not tear them down.

How do you demonstrate value to someone? Know – Show – Grow. The first step is *knowing* them. When you spend time getting to know someone you are saying, "You are worth the investment of my time." Another way is through actions - *showing*. Because you value people, you are willing to serve them. One more way to value people is to *grow* them. Help them develop character, values and integrity. You grow them by passing along what you learn and demonstrating it through your life.

Daily Challenge:

1. Who has added value to your life? Was it someone who made you feel important? Take some time to let them know and say thanks.

2. Ask yourself the tough question: Whom have you not valued? Whom have you made feel like a peasant? How can you change that situation?

3. When you are approaching people, how do you view them? Queen of England or peasant?

4. Pick three people and decide how you can know, show or grow them.

5. Start viewing people as "The Queen of England" today and treat them that way – with value.

Character and Friendships

Day 22

FRIENDSHIP

Josh Shipp

*"A real friend is someone who will walk in,
when everybody else walks out."*

*"A true friend will embarrass themselves in public
to make you laugh when you are having a bad day."*
Andy Austin, student, Oklahoma City, Oklahoma

I tell you what - I LOVE PEOPLE! This world is not about money, careers, or social status - it's about PEOPLE! People make the world go around. People make things like *love* and *friendship* possible.

Here is a list of suggestions to becoming a person whom others will enjoy being around:

- Learn to remember names. A person's name is like music to their ears. Ever been in a crowded place, and heard your name? Your ears perk up!
- Be a very easy-going and humble person, so there is no strain or pressure to hang out with you. How often do you or your parents use that fine china from the china cabinet to eat lunch? I am sure very rarely, probably - more like TUPPERWARE from Wal-Mart.
- Practice liking people. Practice makes IMPROVEMENT.
- Never miss out on an opportunity to congratulate someone on a job well done, or to thank them for doing something nice for you or someone else.

- If you want to find a perfect friend, practice being one to others. Soon after you practice doing this…you will find one.
- Be careful who you hang out with…you may begin to act like them.
- STAY AWAY FROM GOSSIP. If someone talks bad about others behind their backs, what are they saying about you when you are gone?
- SMILE to at LEAST ten people you *do not know* every day.
- Be a friend to someone at your school who may not have many friends.
- Respect and be sensitive to other people's feelings.
- Have fun with life! Make the ordinary EXTRAORDINARY!
- This is the MOST important one. ALWAYS ask, "Is there anything I can do for you?" Never miss out on an opportunity to serve someone else.

Practice these principles in your daily life. It will make all the difference in the world.

Day 23

LAYING DOWN YOUR LIFE...FOR A FRIEND

Bobby Petrocelli

*"To the world you could be just one person,
but to one person YOU COULD BE THE WORLD!"*

Jessica was a beautiful 17-year old high school senior. Two days before prom, she rushed home excitedly to show her mother her new haircut. This wasn't just any haircut - she had gotten it cut, right down to the scalp. Jessica had shaved her head completely bald! Understandably, her mother freaked out. "Jessica, I can't believe you shaved off your beautiful, red curly hair right before your senior prom! What were you thinking? Go to your room! I can't stand looking at you! Wait 'til your father hears about this!"

Jessica ran to her room crying hysterically. "Ma, you don't understand. You just don't understand!"

Two long hours passed before her mother came to Jessica's closed bedroom door where she could hear Jessica sobbing. "Jessica, let me in. I want to talk to you."

After several seconds of awkward anticipation, Jessica reluctantly opened the door and let her mother in. With tears still streaming down her face, Jessica sat on the edge of her bed with her eyes fixated on the carpet patterns below. The ensuing fifteen seconds of silence seemed like an eternity as her mother paced hurriedly back and forth across the floor. Her jaw jutted out in repressed anger as she fumed at Jessica. "What in the w…..What in the w….?" Finally, after two unsuccessful attempts to voice her disbelief, she was able to vocalize her mounting frustration.

"What in the world possessed you to do this? What were you thinking? Who was it?"

Jessica hesitated for a moment, then tearfully lifted her head and in a strained voice, began to reply. "You never gave me a change to explain. It was Mary, Mom. Mary made me do it."

Her mom snapped back, "Well, you give me Mary's phone number right now. I want to speak with her mother and give her a piece of my mind. What kind of girl is Mary? I have never seen something so crazy in my entire life!"

Jessica jumped in saying, "Mom, Mary dropped out of school seven weeks ago. During that time, nobody knew what happened to her, and nobody has been allowed to see her. You see, Mom, she has cancer and has been receiving chemotherapy treatments." Tears began once again to well in her eyes. "Her seven weeks of treatments ended yesterday, and when she finally returned to school today, she was completely bald. No hair on her head at all! No eyebrows, no nothing—not even hair on her arms. She had to wear a red bandanna to cover her head—but people still made fun of her. The boys were especially cruel, calling her 'cue ball, chrome dome, bald eagle,' things like that. My heart broke for her. I decided right then and there that I didn't care how I looked in my prom picture. I wanted Mary to know that she would never have to walk through the halls of our school alone. If people were going to make fun of her, they would have to make fun of me too. I decided that I would be there _**for**_ her and I would be there _**with**_ her. I wanted her to also know that somebody loved her. And that somebody would be me!"

Jessica understands one of the most important principles of life; the further she gets from herself and the further she gets from her own needs, the closer she gets to the heart of serving others! The world around us tells us to look out only for ourselves. It's all about me, me, me, me, me - I'm all that! We have to be willing to be unselfish and focused on others. Those who are servants first are the greatest!

Daily Challenge:

1. Do you possess the courage of Jessica?

2. Would you allow yourself to be humiliated if it meant that you would be doing something great for somebody else?

3. Are you willing to pay that stiff of a price?

4. What kinds of things can you do today or in the next week that might mean laying down your life or your pride for some else?

Character and Love

Day 24

TAKING A STAND TIME AND AGAIN

Jason Palmisano

"If you don't stand for something, you will fall for anything."

As a sophomore at Melbourne High School, I was on the football team. Of course we had a cheerleading squad. One of our cheerleaders was Teri, a senior. You can imagine how surprised I was when I learned that Teri told her friends to tell my friends to tell me that she liked me. I was electrified to say the least. In response, I told my friends, to tell her friends, to tell Teri that I liked her back. Next thing I know, I'm getting a note from Teri through this same mail chain asking me if I wanted to meet her at a particular party after Friday night's football game. I checked the box that read "yes" and sent the note back through the same route.

Since I could not yet drive, I arranged for my big sister Lisa to drive me. Teri and I hit it off great at the party. We talked until I got the nod from my big sis. The nod meant it was time to go. I said goodbye to Teri and headed out the door. As I stepped outside, Teri hooked my arm and dragged me to the side of the house where it was real dark. She then proceeded to get real close to me and said, "How about you and me getting together?" I replied, "Teri, we're together now." "No, No, No!" she said, "I mean how about you and me, you know, getting together?" When I realized what she meant, I didn't quite know how to respond. I pleaded the Fifth, extricated myself from her grasp and sprinted for my sister's car.

On the drive home I thought about Teri's proposition. After all, she was a senior cheerleader and I was just a sophomore. Then I thought, "One day I'll be married. I want my future wife to know that I was a young man with character and was committed to her even before I knew her." I shared my thoughts with Teri, but she wasn't buying the "Leave it to Beaver" routine. She began to put more and more pressure on me to have sex. The more pressure she put on me, the more I resisted. I was actually having fun with it.

Then one morning while getting my books at my locker I heard the rumor. My buddy said, "Aren't you and Teri still dating?" "As far as I know" I replied. "Well, rumor has it that Teri got together with so an so and had sex." I thought I'd better ask Teri to get the real story. You know how true rumors can be. I approached Teri jokingly about it, but she wasn't laughing. She confirmed the rumor to be true. She, in fact, cheated on me because I would not have sex with her. That was my last conversation with Teri. We were through. I felt betrayed and walked away angry. But as the day went on and I reflected over all that happened I became encouraged. I stood up for what I believed to be right and true. I didn't let peer pressure, and others telling me I was missing out, change my mind. I passed up a cheap thrill and gained more strength to stand up for what was right. Yes, I paid a small price, but the rewards of making the stand were well worth it. Just ask my wife. She sure does appreciate hearing this story when I speak on the issue.

Remember, a strong character is built by standing up for what is right, time and time again.

Day 25

"What am I waiting for?"

Waiting for the BEST Sex
Gina Waegele

Perhaps the most difficult area for teens to be patient in is in the area of sex. We hear from the media, friends and other sources that sex is great. So, why do some people say you should wait until you are married?

Let me illustrate. You are in elementary school and it is a week before Christmas. Your mom is taking a nap and you know exactly where the presents are hidden. Not having any patience to wait until Christmas Day, you decide to take a peek. You want to make sure she got you the toys you wanted. (I've even gone to the extreme of unwrapping a present and then re-wrapping it in hopes that my mom would not find out. She never found out - until now as she reads this – sorry Mom!)

Sure enough, your first item on the Christmas list is there. You are excited, but as you put it back and leave the room, you are disappointed and worried. First, you can't play with it until next week; second you went behind your mom's back; third you are hoping that she won't find out. If she finds out, you know she will take it back. On Christmas Day, you open the gift and sure you are excited to finally play with it, but you have to fake the excitement on your face so your mom won't guess that you looked. The present is great, but the surprise and joy of getting it has been ruined.

Like the Christmas gift, when you have sex before marriage, it can be good and you may even enjoy having sex. The problem is, when having sex outside a committed marriage relationship, most people feel regret. They are worried if their boyfriend or girlfriend will leave them, if they are pregnant, or if they have a sexually transmitted disease. If you are in high school, you are more than likely not going to marry the person you are sleeping with. Eventually, it will lead to a more painful break-up because you have bonded sexually.

Who tells you to wait to have sex? Usually parents, teachers, religious leaders and other people who are in authority. What is their motivation? They love you.[1]

What kind of qualities do virgins have? They are leaders. They can stand up against peer pressure. They are confident, goal oriented, self-controlled and patient. Who wouldn't want to marry someone with those qualities?

Guess who is having the best sex? A study out of the University of Chicago found that married couples in monogamous relationships are having the most sex and are the most sexually satisfied.[3] Now that makes sex something worth saving for marriage!

Ultimately a solid marriage relationship is built from two individuals who have solid character. By making the choice to save sex until marriage, you are developing patience, self-control, perseverance, endurance and many other positive character traits. Qualities such as these make a person attractive, especially to those with the same qualities. These attributes contribute to a stable and lasting marriage. If you can stay committed to avoid one of the most tempting and attractive risk behaviors as a teen and/or single person, the smaller temptations will be *a lot* easier to avoid.

Daily Challenge:
1. How would it benefit you personally to save sex for marriage?

References:
1. WAIT Training, Used with Permission
2. WAIT Training, Used with Permission
3. Time Magazine: October 17, 1994. Pages 62-70

Day 26

"I'VE ALREADY HAD SEX!" IS IT TOO LATE?

Gina Waegele

*"Our greatest glory is not never falling,
but rising every time we fall."*
- Confucius

"You are worth the wait," Carrie said, trying to convince a teenage girl she was mentoring.

Tina's eyes welled up with tears. As a teenage mother of a toddler and with another baby on the way, Tina had never heard those words. She never placed enough value on herself to save herself sexually until marriage. Once she lost her virginity and especially after she had her first baby, she didn't think she could ever start over.

No matter what choices you have made regarding sex, drugs, alcohol and/or other risky behaviors, you have the opportunity to start over. Whatever path you take in life, you will fall from time to time. You will make mistakes. Whether your mistakes are large or small, your response to failure determines your character. If you don't even acknowledge you failed, or don't try to learn from failure, you won't learn and grow as a person.

The heartache that goes along with having sex when not in a committed marriage relationship, can, many times, be worse than the shock of finding out you're pregnant as a teen. Tina experienced a broken heart not just because she got pregnant, but because she was used and mistreated by her partner. By making the decision to save sex until marriage, she is saving herself from a broken heart and the potential of another unplanned pregnancy, not to mention contracting a sexually transmitted disease.

How do we rise when we fall? Rising means learning why you fell in the first place, and then picking yourself up off the ground and stepping out to a new challenge. Because you have learned from your mistakes, you may not fall as hard, or as far, the next time.

First, be willing to admit that you have made a mistake. Be open to constructive criticism and take a look at how you can improve yourself daily. Then, if you can learn anything from your failure, it wasn't a total failure. Why is Tina about to have her second baby as a teenager? She engaged in sex when she wasn't ready to deal with the consequences of having children. Not to mention the fact that she has to deal with a broken heart.

Second, make a written commitment of what you plan on changing about your life. Then, share it with a friend or family member that will hold you accountable. In the area of sex before marriage, a written commitment is very effective.

Third, make amends with anyone who may have been involved with your mistake. If you were offensive or didn't treat them the way they should be treated, do what you can to make peace. If they refuse to forgive you or cooperate, just know you have tried and move on.

Fourth, if you are around people who are involved in the behaviors you are trying to avoid, stop hanging around them. Hang around people who will lift you up and support you in making healthy choices for your life. If Tina continues to date men that do not share her commitment of waiting to have sex until marriage, it will be a lot more difficult to keep her commitment.

By becoming abstinent until marriage, Tina is rising from the times she fell. She will become a stronger more confident woman and what man of character doesn't like that in a woman?

When you rise every time you fall, you are humbled and are developing perseverance, while becoming wiser. Next time you fall, I challenge you to rise and see how you can better yourself from falling! In the area of sexual purity, you can make the decision to start over today with the new information you have! It is never too late to make better choices!

Daily Challenge:
1. When did you "fall the hardest"?
2. How did you "rise" from your fall, or did you ever "rise"?
3. What can you do in the future when you "fall"?
4. Have you been sexually active?
5. How will you better yourself from past sexual choices?

Day 27

KEEP THOSE HORMONES UNDER CONTROL!

Gina Waegele

It was another Saturday morning and Jim woke up with the same headache and the same smell of alcohol on him, but this morning, he felt different. Next to him laid a girl named Shelly. Shelly was known at school for being "easy." Jim went home feeling terrible and it wasn't because of his headache. All of his friends talked about how great sex was, but Jim barely remembered a thing that had happened. Even if he did remember the details, there was nothing special about his first time. It was on the floor with a girl that had slept with most of his friends. He wished he could go back and change what happened.

"How did it come to this?" Jim asked himself and then thought through everything that happened. "I shouldn't have been talking to her. Everyone ends up sleeping with her. Maybe if I weren't drunk it wouldn't have happened. I shouldn't have even been drinking. Maybe I shouldn't have even gone to the party." Jim continued to go over the many actions he felt he "shouldn't have done." He traced it all the way back to when should have stayed home to do his homework rather than going out with his new group of friends.

It may sound extreme that skipping one homework assignment caused him to sleep with a girl, but it is a lack of self-control in small areas in our lives that leads to lack of self-control in the areas where we can suffer larger consequences.

An experiment conducted at Stanford University, known as the "marshmallow test," showed that self-control has an impact on future success. Philip Peake, a psychiatrist tested the self-control of four year-olds by sitting at a table with a marshmallow in front of them. He told them that if they can sit in the room with the marshmallow and not eat it, they could have two when he came back. Some children were able to wait and some were not able to wait. He followed the children and fourteen years later, he found that the ones who were able to wait had an average of 210 points higher on their SAT's. By the time they were in their late twenties, those who waited had developed closer relationships with people and were more dependable and responsible.[1]

The Character Training Institute defines self-control as, "Rejecting my own desires and doing what is right." Just because it "feels" good doesn't mean it is right. For Jim, skipping his homework "felt" good, but it wasn't right.

Practice having self-control in smaller areas where it is easy. Try making sure all of your homework is done before turning on the television or talking on the phone. Avoid buying something that you want, but don't need. When you develop self-control in smaller areas of your life, you will have an easier time using self-control when you are faced with choices that have more serious consequences, like pre-marital sex, tobacco, alcohol and other drugs.

Daily Challenge:
1. How can you practice self-control in your daily life?

Reference
1. Goleman, Daniel. <u>Working with Emotional Intelligence</u>. Bantam Books, 1998. 78-80. Data collection

and analysis conducted by Philip Peake, psychiatrist at Smith College.

Day 28

WAIT! DON'T CROSS THIS LINE!

Gina Waegele

Tim heard his friends talk all the time at school about how great their sex lives were. He had always been told at church and by his parent to wait until he was married, but he didn't know anyone who waited. His girlfriend wasn't even a virgin. One night they were alone at her house and had sex. They weren't even planning to have sex. "It just happened," Tim thought, "How did it just happen?" They had sex one more time and the relationship ended a week later. Tim felt terrible. "If I wouldn't have had sex with her, I wouldn't feel so bad."

"It just happened," is a common phrase people use. They never planned to have sex, but "one thing led to another." How can you avoid "one thing leading to the other?"

First, you may be asking if it is even possible to save sex until marriage. It is possible and realistic, but it takes work. Being home alone with your significant other, like Tim was alone with his girlfriend, is not a good place to be if you are committed to saving sex for marriage! By setting boundaries and planning ahead you will develop your character and save yourself from making a mistake.

The following is a short list of boundaries that you can set today!

- Tell your date up front how far you will go physically. Don't wait until the "heat of the moment" to decide how far you will go.
- Plan your date before you go out. When you don't know what to do for the last two hours of your date, it is easy to find "something to do" especially if your date is attractive!
- Riding out to the middle of nowhere to look at the stars may be romantic, but it is an easy way to put yourself in a position of going too far physically.
- Don't be home alone or in a bedroom alone. Most teens who are having sex are doing so after school in an empty house with their pants around their ankles in fear of parents coming home. How completely unromantic!
- Date someone with the same standards that you have about sex.
- Add to this list and have a friend or family member hold you accountable!

If you have chosen to save sex until marriage, like many others, you may be wondering, "how far can I go?" The Medical Institute of Sexual Health Today defines true abstinence as "a contraceptive without a failure rate" and "a lifestyle." It does not include periodic abstinence, mutual masturbation, outer-course, genital contact, oral and anal sex.[1] This definition is based on potential health risks by being involved in these sexual behaviors.

Setting boundaries in the area of sex will help develop character in your life. By setting boundaries in an area where you are at risk for severe consequences, you are placing value and worth on yourself.

Daily Challenge:
    1. What are the benefits of setting boundaries in my relationships?
    2. What boundaries can I set in my dating relationships?

Reference:
    1. <u>Medical Institute Sexual Health Today</u>. Slide Program, Lecture Notes and Supplemental Materials. 1996. Page 179, slide 81.

SECTION NINE

Perseverance and Character

Day 29

ROCKBOTTOMVILLE

Sam Glenn

Sometimes in life we don't understand the trials we go through. We have no clue what tomorrow will bring. We feel prayed out and hopeless. It seems that we have lost all the energy to try again. We wrestle with anxiety, frustration, defeat, fear, worry, anger, resentment, and all that junk. We've journeyed for what seems to be a million miles, only to end up in the darkest town in the world - Rockbottomville. So what's next? Where do we go, what do we think, what do we do?

Let me tell you, I have been to Rockbottomville. I got there and, figuring that this was as good as it was going to get, I settled in, bought property, had pity parties, and went day to day in gloom and doom. I learned quickly that the sun doesn't shine very bright in Rockbottomville.

The greatest moment I had while living in Rockbottomville was when I realized that *I did not have to stay*! I could get up at anytime and leave. It was my choice to go. Nobody was keeping me there but me. It was my own actions and attitudes keeping me there. I put myself there with my doubting beliefs, my lack of positive actions, and a complaining attitude. I learned that everyone in Rockbottomville was just like me. It was a crowded town. New people came to live there everyday.

Every now and then, you would witness something absolutely amazing. Someone would stand up in the middle of the town and shout with a booming voice for all to hear, "I am not living like this ANY MORE!!" The crowd would hurl insults at them and do everything they could to get them to stay (misery likes company, you know). But, they would rise up, ignore the insults, and leave it all behind. I guess they got tired of Rockbottomville. It was fear that led them there, but courage that led them out. What did that person have to think that allowed them to get up and leave? What did they have to believe? What was the breaking point or turning point that caused them to change and get up? How did they do it and why? The answer is this: they discovered something.

There is something in all of us, something we are all born with – the understanding that at any moment in time we too can change, think new thoughts, establish better beliefs, take new actions, adopt a new attitude about life, and live the best that life has to offer.

Daily Challenge:

1. The way out of a rut is find something to be thankful for, list things you can be thankful for?

2. What excuses are holding you back from your best?

3. What is one action you can take today that will move you in the direction of your dreams or goals?

Day 30

PROBLEMS

Josh Shipp

*"Problems are like GAS.
If you don't relieve yourself...you'll explode!"*
–Josh Shipp

*"Character is something learned by experiences,
both positive and negative."*
–Natalie Owens, student Traer, Iowa.

The other day I decided to wash my car. It's been a while since I've washed it and since the weather was so nice, I figured, "What a great opportunity!" I spent around an hour or so washing it and cleaning it up. After all my hard work, it looked FANTASTIC!! The time I spent cleaning my vehicle was well worth it. A great investment of my time!

However, somewhere on my way home from the car wash a flock of birds, which probably just ate a lot of bean burritos or something, gracefully relieved themselves on my CLEAN car! This may have happened to you before. Or maybe every time you wash your car...IT RAINS.

Similar situations happen to us in our own lives. Just when things seem to be going our way...some problem arises. Something rains on our parade.

This should be nothing more than a challenge to you, a challenge to make it through the problem that life just handed you and look at it as an opportunity. Opportunities for you to make something GREAT happen! Problems are going to arise. This you cannot control, but you CAN CONTROL how you deal with them. Make the best out of every problem that arises in your life. Mike Patrick says, "The problem isn't the issue, the issue is how you deal with the problem." How are you going to deal with the problems that life deals you?

PROBLEMS are:

Present. Don't ever think that you are the only one who has to deal with problems. Each and every one of us deals with problems EVERY DAY.

Rude. Problems will arise unannounced. They don't call to schedule an appointment or see if we are ready for them. Be ready for them and be ready to deal with them with a positive attitude.

Opportunities. Once you overcome a problem you are now in a great position to help others.

Blessings. They open up doors that we usually do not go through. This will make us better people.

Lessons. Each new problem will be our teacher. The problems in our life make us stronger and wiser.

Everywhere. No place or person is excluded from problems. Chances are someone you know is dealing with similar problems.

Messages. They warn us about potential disaster. Who knows what would of happened if you wouldn't have been stuck in traffic. You might have been the accident.

Solvable. No problem that arises in your life is without a solution. Don't be bashful about asking for help from others.

Tips for Dealing with Day-to-Day Problems

- **Be positive!** You can't control problems, but you CAN control your attitude towards them. Stay Positive!

- **Don't procrastinate...REGULATE!** If you put a white sheet over that lime green couch, the couch is still lime green right? Don't try to cover up your problems and pretend your problems are not there. You cannot FIX what you don't acknowledge.

- **TALK.** Talk about your problems with people you trust. Talk to a friend, family member, counselor, teacher, coach, pastor, mentor, etc. What you don't talk out, you act out. Know someone who is causing a lot of trouble? Chances are they are having some life problems. Lend an ear to them.

Day 31

THE HEART OF A CHAMPION

Frank Shelton

"Champions never ask what is the least they can do."
"The difference between a champ and a chump is U!"

I recall a story of a freshman in college who stuck a "V" on the door of his dorm room. People initially passed by and thought nothing of it. About mid-semester some friends began to inquire what the "V" stood for? One friend said: "I think it means he wants to be on the varsity." Another quipped: "No, I think it means he is a virgin!" The student despite the criticism remained calm and never answered their silly slurs.

The summer finally rolled around and his friends were surprised to see him tack up the "V" on the front of his door the following school year. Again, the jokes persisted and he remained steadfast. Ironically, he did this all four years of college and on graduation day he finally told his entire class what the "V" stood for. He was the valedictorian of his college and he shared with them that since high school he had a dream to graduate at the top of his college class. He posted the "V" on his door to remind him at the close of each evening and the beginning of each day that he would have to walk and talk like a valedictorian if he wanted to receive the prestigious award.

The Notre Dame football team has a tradition that at every practice and every home game they tap a sign that has been affixed to the wall in the locker room for decades. The players touch the sign right before exiting the locker room to walk onto the field where dozens of game day memories have transpired. The sign simply says: "PLAY LIKE A CHAMPION TODAY!"

It has been said: "Our outlook determines our outcome!" What we *dream* yesterday and what we *dwell* on today is what we will *do* tomorrow. Friend, no one is an "over night" success! There is no such thing because that singer, speaker, athlete, businessman, etc. has been practicing in private for years before finally being applauded in public. The question is how bad do you want to succeed? Nothing worth having comes easy. The road to success is a journey not a destination. Also, the path to prosperity is paved with many setbacks. However, the trials and tragedies you encounter now will be your testimony of your triumphs in the future! It has been said: "Winners never quit and quitters never win."

Daily Challenge:
1. What do you want out of life? Make a list of 10 things you want to achieve out of life or see happen.
2. What are you willing to do to get what you want?

Day 32

NEVER GIVE UP ON YOUR DREAMS

Frank Shelton

*"If a dream dies, don't die with it.
It means dream a new dream!"*

"I have a dream!" – Martin Luther King

I have noticed a common theme in the heart of champions. They are *persevering and persistent.* A young African-American was cut from his varsity basketball team his tenth grade year in a rural school in Wilmington, North Carolina. He was devastated and he ran as fast as he could to his home and cried for hours on his pillow. He wanted more than anything to play on the basketball team. However, his pride never took precedent over his dedication. He wanted to play so much that he knew it would "kill" him if he could not at least be around his peers on the team.

Without hesitation, he begged the coach to at least let him ride the bus with the players and he would serve as the ball boy. He loved the smell of the gym. He nearly idolized the players on the squad and practiced harder on his personal time than anyone in his school. The following year, he tried again to make the squad and he was successful the second time around.

He went on to receive a full scholarship to the University of North Carolina and hit the winning jumper to win the NCAA Championship over Patrick Ewing and the

Georgetown Hoyas. He went on to dominate the NBA and changed the sneaker industry by his billion dollar sales with Nike.

His initial setback was the greatest thing that ever happened to him because if he did not know the pain of defeat he would never have soared to "Air Jordan" heights. Setbacks either "make" or "break" an individual and this is what separates the wheat from the chaff, the men from the boys; the cubic zirconia's from the diamond. I love the quote: "Never fear *pressure* because it is pressure that turns a lump of coal into a diamond!"

Arguably the greatest leader of America's political system encountered enormous losses before occupying the Oval Office. Abraham Lincoln encountered 11 personal and public defeats in 27 short years before taking residence in the White House.

Since childhood, some of my favorite super heroes were Superman and Rocky Bal boa. In eighth grade, I entered a Rambo contest and made a bet with my godmother, Judy Henderson that if I won I would take her and she said if she won she would take me as her guest. The trip would include round trip airfare from Washington DC to Hollywood, California to spend the weekend with Sylvester Stallone. God works in mysterious ways because my godmother won and she honored her promise and took me as her guest to meet my favorite actor. For a 12 year-old kid this was a dream come true. I have an autograph from "Rocky" and I have the identical red, white and blue boxing trunks framed at home that he made famous in the movies. I love the spirit of "Rocky." Millions of movie fans around the globe did not relate and revere "Rocky" because he never lost, but because he never quit! It is not wrong for being knocked down, it is wrong to stay on the canvas of life and not get up. In life, in order to be victorious, when the last bell sounds are we standing or sitting? This is the heart of a champion and this makes all the difference between a loser and a leader, a spectator and a sportsman, a dreamer or a doer.

Daily Challenge:

1. Was there ever a time you felt like giving up? Why?

2. Is there a time you felt like giving up, but didn't? What pushed you on to not give up?

3. What should you do or can you do if you feel like giving up?

4. What happens when people give up on their dreams?

5. What happens when people don't give up on their dreams?

Day 33

A Little Extra Makes A Big Difference

Frank Shelton

"Inch by inch…it's a cinch!"

A young oil executive was just starting the business. His equipment was second hand, but his determination was first rate. He would go to the oil field where experienced oil companies had previously dug for oil with their million dollar equipment and once they pulled out to move on to another location, he would try with his used and abused equipment. Ironically, he once began to dig where another company quit and he hit the second largest oil jackpot in Texas history! How? Because he chose to dig an additional three feet! Friends, "winners never quit and quitters never win."

There are times when you will feel like throwing in the towel, doubt your abilities, question your worth and just want to give up. That is what you will experience in the pursuit of your greatness and dreams. It's just a part of it. There might be times when you will be tired and worn out and wonder if what you are doing is even worth it. There is a dynamic saying, "A little extra makes a big difference." It's the little things that make the big difference. Ever seen a racehorse win a race by a hair? Ever see a million dollar baseball player and a hundred thousand dollar baseball player? Do you know the difference? It may be one extra hit at bat. Not much of a difference, but the results of that difference are dramatic. It's the little things that add up to make the big difference.

Is there something in your life that needs that little extra? What dramatic difference would there be if you applied just a little extra effort in certain areas of your life? Maybe a little extra effort towards your character, your dreams, goals, relationships, work, or school. It all makes a difference. Don't give up when your hardest times hit, its when things seem wrong that we must not quit. What benefits are there to quitting on our dreams or ourselves? Not many. What benefits are there to pushing ourselves just a little bit more. You think about that.

Mother Teresa on her deathbed remarked: "God did not call me to be FAMOUS but FAITHFUL." Faithfulness is commitment despite the odds or circumstances. It's the little extra we need to make the big difference, even when we think no progress is being made. If you are patient, persistent and persevering then you will be both productive and prosperous. The last four letters of *American* spell "I Can". With a little extra effort you CAN do anything! You may be down, but you are not out, you may be discouraged, but you are not defeated and you may feel alone but you are not because your family, friends and your Creator are all pulling for you.

Daily Challenge:

1. Is there an area of your life that needs extra effort - goals, relationships, work, dreams, school?

Define the extra effort you can do that will make a difference in your life.

SECTION TEN

Character for Life

Day 34

SEIZE THE DAY!

Sam Glenn

"Choose not to live by chance, but to live by purpose."
Don't look back and say, " I wish I had or I wish I did."

I once heard a story about a boy who fell through ice and began to drown. A man came along and amazingly rescued the boy. The boy said, "I don't know how to repay you for saving my life." The man said, "Make sure you live life in a way that it was worth saving!"

You have one life, make sure your life is one worth saving. If you live in that way, it will be the most rewarding and fulfilling journey ever.

Take wisdom and apply it to your life. Take challenges and let them grow you, not destroy you. If you are not willing to change and get over things that have happened to you in the past, then you will never know the essence and fullness of what life can offer you.

You are not here to fritter away your precious hours when you have the ability to accomplish so much. You are not here to just be a survivor, you are here to live a victorious life. I believe there is something within us all that desires to make the most of life, but often something holds us back. What and who are you blaming for not living life to the fullest? What excuses are holding you back?

Daily Challenge:
1. This is your day, a day that can never be lived again. Think about how you use your time. Do you

waste it watching TV or do you live your life with meaning and purpose?

2. Take a few moments to think about where your time is being spent.

3. What can you do to better manage your time so that you will be seizing the day?

Day 35

CREATE YOUR OWN LEGACY

Sam Glenn

Yesterday is history, tomorrow is a mystery and today is gift. "Your life is what you desire it to be." – S. Glenn

Ask yourself this: "If I could be remembered for anything, what would it be?"

When your time is up on earth, what will people remember of you? What are you doing to make your life count now, today and for the future of others to come?

Most called him Richard Albertson and for the short time that I knew him, I called him Grandpa. My grandpa was a giant, both in physical stature and with his attitude. He could make almost anyone smile and he had a special gift. Grandpa was always known for saying the words, *"Holy buckets!"* That was his line. Whenever we drove in his old red pick up truck, it did not matter who you were, he would get you to sing with him, *"You are my sunshine...my only sunshine, you make me happy when skies are gray...how much I love you, so please don't take my sunshine away."* What an impact that had on my attitude. As corny as what it seemed to be at the time, it put a smile on my face and made me feel real good!

Grandpa had his own special way with people. He had a touch of joy that he left in people's hearts. He always seemed ready to go the extra mile and help others out. If it were in his capacity, he would do whatever he could for you. That was his nature, or one that he acquired over the years of learning and life lessons. Everywhere I went with him, it seemed like everyone knew him, and Gramps had a kind word to offer up. My grandpa was very approachable. He could talk to strangers like he'd known them for years. He always expressed interest in people.

Gramps was a nice guy, but I do remember that if you ever got out of line, he would let you know it, *"Holy buckets!"* I will always remember him as the giant that could touch the ceiling with his hands, play the organ and get you dancing, take you fishing in a heartbeat, and just loved to spend time with people. This is how I will always remember him. He didn't have a big organization that was out to change the world, he didn't go speak to large groups, and he didn't even have that much money to give. But what he did have, he used and gave, and that was enough to make a difference. A lesson we can all live by. He, like all of us, had a uniqueness within him, an impression to leave on the world, something to leave footprints in the sand...not butt prints.

In 1989, my grandpa passed away due to lung cancer. He was sick for a long time and it always made me sad to see him breathing from an oxygen tank. In his last days, I remember seeing this giant of a man looking worn out with very little life left in him. In those last days, I learned how priceless our time is here and with others. It's but a flicker!

My grandfather's death was my first real experience of losing someone close. At his funeral, many people showed up - some I knew and many I did not know. I listened to people tell stories about grandpa and some even engaged in laughter. Some people wore expressions of happiness while others remembered him in tears. Watching all this made me realize something about life. When people laugh, cheer, celebrate, give thanks, or remember you in tears at your funeral, **it is not merely because you are gone, but because you have touched their life with your greatness.** My grandpa touched many lives with who he was, the way he lived and what he gave. When you touch other people's lives, life seems to give you back rewards beyond words, beyond money, and almost always beyond expression. It goes to the treasure chest in our heart.

We all have something to give that can make a difference. Each of us can lend a hand, give a hug, give of our time, make a phone call, get involved, clean toilets, pray with someone, do something. When we do that, do you know what? **It all makes a difference!** Who you are makes a difference. If anyone has left you out in the dark or made you feel worthless and useless, I have some news for you - they are wrong! They lied to you. They misled you. They are too busy to see your greatness deep down. I have some new and good news for you: what you do and who you are for as long as you walk this planet does make a difference in this world. Don't keep your gifts locked up. Open up and let the colors of who you are and what you have to give touch the life of another. **When you give of yourself, you make footprints in the sands of life.**

Daily Challenge:

1. Write down what you want people to remember about you.

2. What do you desire your legacy to be?

3. What would you like to do that could make a difference for others?

Day 36

HOW TO GET WHAT YOU WANT OUT OF LIFE

Josh Shipp

"It's my responsibility to become the person I want to be."
—Manisha Bahl, student Stanford University

"Leadership is defined in five short words... HELPING OTHERS ACHIEVE THEIR GOALS." – Josh Shipp

Have you ever eaten SPAM? You know, "The other white meat." If you have, allow me to say that you have more courage than I do. If you are a SPAM lover please pardon me for the next few moments, while I poke fun at SPAM. (a.k.a. "Slime Passed As Meat") The thing that confuses me the most is...what exactly is SPAM? To me, it looks like a jello/meat mixture. SPAM actually wiggles! Real meat DOESN'T wiggle! Then there is that slime layer on the top. What IS that? To me, it's a warning label that says: "WARNING YOU ARE ABOUT TO EAT THE MOST HORRID THING AVAILABLE ON EARTH."

However disgusting it may seem, SPAM does suggest something positive for us. It suggests a formula for setting goals in our own lives.

"Huh?" Let me explain...

108

SPAM: The Recipe for Goal Setting in Your Own Life

S- *Specific*: Your goals in life must be specific. For example don't just say, "I want to be involved at my school." Say, "I am going to be involved in student council and the multi-cultural club." When you decide what your goals are going to be WRITE THEM DOWN. Make several copies... put them in places where you will see them daily. For example: your car, bedroom, bathroom, in the refrigerator, etc. Also give a copy to a friend and ask them to hold you accountable for your goals.

P- *Planned*: You must have a course of ACTION for your goals. Otherwise, how are you ever going to accomplish them? "If you fail to plan, you plan to fail." Set up a strategy for accomplishing your goals, and then go AFTER them full force.

A- *Achievable*: Be realistic with your goals. Understand what you are capable of accomplishing. Set YOUR OWN STANDARDS. Don't get caught up in what the world expects of you. Set your own expectations...and NEVER GIVE UP until you reach them. Believe in what you CAN do. "Whether you think you can or you CANNOT, you are RIGHT!"

M- *Made:* ACCOMPLISH your goals. Set out after your goals with a burning passion and don't stop until you achieve them. You know what you are capable of! Sometimes it's easy to just give into others negative thinking of us. STAY POSITIVE! You know you can do it, don't worry about what others think.

May **SPAM** be with you!

Daily Challenge:
1. What are some of your future goals?
2. Run your list of goals through the SPAM recipe.

Day 37

BOLDLY GOING WHERE NO MAN HAS GONE BEFORE

Ben Glenn

"Chalk artists are cool!"
"Every choice you make is taking you somewhere."

In 1994, I was sitting in my dorm room at Anderson University, deliberating a difficult choice; stay at school and complete my teaching degree or pack it all up into my decaying 1986 Plymouth Lancer and get on the road to be a speaker full-time. Knowing what I know now would have made it an easy decision, but of course I had no knowledge of what my future would hold and so was struggling with all kinds of doubts and fears.

Staying at school made a lot more sense. I was half way through my third year as an education major. I'd even done some practical classroom training. I could picture it with ease. I'm settled in a nice suburb of Chicago, dissecting frogs and discussing the properties of chlorophyll with my students. Summers off for camping and fishing. A little basketball coaching on the side to stay in shape. It could be a life of comfort and predictability. Yet, something in this picture just didn't fit. I couldn't quite put my finger on it, but I had a sense that beyond this predictable life that was mine for the taking, was something far greater, far more exciting and far more fulfilling. Unfortunately, I wasn't all that convinced that being a chalk artist and a speaker would necessarily bring me closer to this greater, more exciting and more fulfilling life.

Let's start with the fact that I had no clients. Nobody knew that somewhere, amidst the corn fields of Indiana was this guy by the name of Ben Glenn, messing around with chalk, hoping one day to make a difference. I also wasn't that good of an artist. Proof of my early artistic attempts can be found at several churches and camps around the mid-west – I won't be the one telling you which ones, though!

One day, I was sitting around mulling over my dilemma and I realized that the only way that I would ever find out what I was capable of, was for me to get off my duff and **take a bold step in the direction of the unknown.**

Mind you being bold is not the same as being reckless. I had spent many an hour contemplating my future – all the pros and cons, the pitfalls and the benefits. I wasn't just making a rash decision. In my heart, I knew what I wanted to do, but I was letting fear of the unknown and also fear of what others would say, get in the way of making a decision. **Being bold means having confidence that what you are doing or saying is true, right and just.** Just knowing the right thing to do and say is not enough though, you must act on it!

Do yourself a favor and DO the right thing. Be bold!

Daily Challenge:
1. Is there a situation in your life where you know what the right thing to do or say is, but you're holding back because of fear?

Day 38

YOUR ATTITUDE DETERMINES YOUR ALTITUDE

Jason Palmisano

*"If you don't like the output in your life,
you must change the input." – Zig Ziglar*

"What goes in will come out. Good stuff in, good stuff out."

Have you ever noticed that sometimes life doesn't turn out the way you hoped it would? My family and I were getting ready to leave a restaurant. We had finished the meal, paid the bill and were now pushing back from the table. As we stood up, my two-year-old boy Michael said, "Daddy, I want to go on your neck." He loves to ride up high on my shoulders, and of course, I love to have him there. So, I leaned down to scoop my boy off the ground and thrust him into the air. There was one small problem. I failed to notice the high-speed paddle fan right above our heads! The next sound I heard was, thud, thud, thud, thud, as my little boy's head went into the fan. He had golf ball size knots all over his little head. I felt awful! Some dad! That sure didn't turn out the way I'd hoped.

Forrest Gump said it best: "Mama always told me life is like a box of chocolates. You never know what you're going to get." That is so true. You and I can try our best and hope for the best, but the fact still remains... sometimes life doesn't turn out the way we hope. Maybe it's the divorce your parents went through, or maybe you didn't make the team or the grades, or a tragedy has happened, or your best friend dumped you for another. Any number of circumstances can take us by surprise and throw our lives in turmoil. So what do you do? How do you handle it?

When faced with these rainy days, some people allow their lives to become unraveled and they never recover. Others bounce back and become stronger. What makes the difference? I have found that in every circumstance the unmistakable, unquestionable difference is our ATTITUDE! I don't know your background or what you've been through, but I can promise you this: **with a positive attitude, the absolute very best in your life is yet to come.**

Recently my wife, Wendy, and I went through one of life's rainy days. It was March 26, 2001. We were so excited because we were about to find out if the baby that we were expecting was a boy or a girl. This would be our fourth child in four years! (My wife and I have been busy!) During the ultrasound procedure, the doctor showed us the hands, the fingers, then the toes. Yep, it's a boy - no mistaking that. Suddenly, the doctor got quiet and started examining the ultrasound image very closely. He said, "We need to talk. Your baby isn't developing like a normal baby." He showed us that our little boy's spine hadn't closed all the way and his head appeared larger than normal.

Our son had spina bifida and hydrocephalus (too much water in the brain). We learned that our boy would need to have two major surgeries within the first forty-eight hours of his life. The severity of his condition could not be determined, but the doctor mentioned that there was a chance that he'd be wheelchair-bound for life, among other things. Then he said, "Maybe you ought to consider terminating this pregnancy." No way! Even though this wasn't turning

out the way we'd hoped, we would have this baby no matter what!

Here is what I learned through the experience. We
could not control our boy's condition nor could we control
what the doctor suggested we do with him. The only thing
we had any say in was our attitude. We decided to look at
all the positives in our lives - a great marriage, three healthy
kids, family support, the facts that our new baby could be
the greatest blessing of our lives and that God would never
give us more than we could handle. By refusing to become
discouraged, we grew stronger. There is incredible power in
a positive attitude and the best part is that you are in control of it. **It's been said that when life rains, learn to carry
your own weather.**

My challenge to you, in your quest of a strong character
is to learn how to have control of your attitude. Always
look for the positives and make the most out of your life
and the circumstances that surround you.

Commitment

Commitment To Character

"You begin to change the world
when you start by changing yourself."

"Whatever it takes in life...you are worth it.
Make a commitment to live your life
in a way that radiates your greatness."

You cannot wish for life to get better. The key to making things better is that **we** have to get better. That starts with our character. This requires personal evaluation, work, thought, choices and change.

I want to challenge you to fill this out. Remember, once you sign it, you must follow through. You are saying that you are a person of your word. If you don't follow through, you only hurt yourself.

Commitment to an Unshakable Character

Today I choose to make decisions as a person of unshakable character. I will take full responsibility for who I am, where I am, and where I am going in life. I know that my future does not resemble my past. I am ready to take my first step toward the making of an unshakable character.

I will change, grow, commit and do whatever it takes to live a life of honor, respect, integrity, purity, excellence, and act on my personal calling.

Signature:_____

Date:_____

Witness:_____

117

118

Sam Glenn

He went from living on his mom's living room floor, broke, depressed and working as a night time janitor to speaking for the Billy Graham Association.

He has spoken to over one million people and to audiences as large as 80,000 people. Sam is the author of six books. His message is unique, different and life changing. Sam's audiences laugh themselves silly as he shares inspirational messages that focus on life skills, character, attitude and life choices.

Sam Glenn	Motivational Presentations
(800) 818-6378	608 S. Washington Ste 101
SamGlenn.com	Naperville, IL 60540

Gina Marie Waegele

Gina brings enthusiasm and excitement to audiences through her energy and attention grabbing demonstrations. In her presentations, Gina shares personal stories of triumph over tragedy as she shares entries from her journal, to personal experiences of domestic violence, to her one-of-a-kind experience as Miss Colorado. Gina is sure to motivate audiences to action whether speaking on relationships, areas of motivation, or self-image.

Resource–FRIENDS FIRST equips youth, families and communities to make healthy life choices by imparting relationship education and promoting the benefits of abstinence until marriage. The FRIENDS FIRST STARS Mentoring Program gives teens the tools to make healthy decisions regarding relationships.

(800) 909-WAIT	Friends First
gina@friendsfirst.org	PO Box 356
www.friendsfirst.org	Longmont, CO 80501

Mark Eiken

Mark Eiken carries a humorous and challenging message that will motivate and inspire people of all ages. He has over 15 years of experience in Student Ministry, Evangelism, Worship and Leadership Development. Mark is a husband, father of three children, and is currently a teaching pastor at Crossroads Community

Church in Naperville, IL. He is available to speak on a wide variety of topics and provide leadership training for students and adults. For more information please call: (630) 551-1705.

Ben Glenn

Ben has been sharing his unique Living Art prorgam since1993. Those who experience Ben leave motivated by his awesome story and energized by his multi-media program. As he combines his expertise and riveting personal experience, Ben never fails to inspire, empower and encourage. He travels internationally sharing his great news to all ages, from all walks of life, in his own enthusiastic and humorous way! Ben is the author of "Big Enough, Finding Faith to Move Mountains" and is the President of Living Art. Ben, his wife and their three dogs reside in Indianapolis, IN.

Living Art
Ben Glenn
5652 Georgetown Rd, pmb 314
Indianapolis, IN 46254

(317)280-1455
fax: (317) 280-1454
(800) 763-2609
www.chalkguy.com

Bobby Petrocelli

The greatest compliment a young person can pay you is that you are REAL! That is the term young people use when describing Bobby Petrocelli. He wants young people all across this nation to know that God's Love is Real too!!! Bobby's zest for life and sincere love for people is communicated through his message. As he combines his expertise and riveting personal experience, he never fails to inspire, empower and encourage the audiences hearing his life story. His message is clear and simple...10 Seconds is all it takes to change a life forever. Bobby is also the author of "Triumph Over Tragedy" and has co-authored four books in the Teen Power series. Through his organization, 10 Seconds, Inc., Bobby is a "man on a mission."-to bring faith, hope and love to all who will hear him.

Bobby Petrocelli
10 Seconds, Inc.
P.O. Box 923
Bellport, NY 11713

(800) 547-7933
www.10seconds.org
tseconds@aol.com

Jeff Canfield

Jeff Canfield is a former police officer, and currently is the pastor of Word of Life Church in Sullivan, Indiana. Jeff is also the author of two books - Life Isn't Rocket Science and A Call to Honor. To contact Jeff call (812) 268-3130, or go to www.canfieldminitries.org.

Rolfe Carawan

Rolfe is passionate, hilarious and refreshingly honest. Drawing from years of rich experience as an athlete, teacher, coach and counselor, Rolfe captivates audiences throughout the nation with his powerful message and practical insights. With wisdom that comes from God's Word alone, Rolfe skillfully addresses the tough issues: alcohol, drugs, sex, depression, teen suicide, gangs, violence and peer pressure. Whether he is speaking at a convention, professional development day, leadership conference, parent seminar or school assembly, Rolfe always leaves a lasting impact. Traveling over 100,000 miles a year, his legacy is thousands of people who have been inspired to live a life of character, competence and compassion.

LifeMatters
20613 6th Ave. SW
Seattle, WA 98166
(800) 258-3966

(206) 870-9109 fax
rolfe@lifematters.net
rolfe@rolfecarawan.com
www.rolfecarawan.com

Jason Palmisano

Jason is passionate, emotional, hilarious. You will laugh and be inspired by this master story teller. Former teacher, coach, and youth pastor, Jason captivates audiences throughout the nation with his father's heart, humor and practical insights. Jason is the author of "The Extra Mile, a 22-day Challenge" and a staff presenter with Living Art. Bringing his unique message of success and leadership, Jason, his wife Wendy, and their four children, live in Palm Bay Florida.

Living Art
Jason Palmisano
5652 Georgetown Rd, pmb 314
Indianapolis, IN 46254

(317)280-1455
fax: (317) 280-1454
(800) 763-2609
www.chalkguy.com

Frank Shelton, Jr.

Frank Shelton, Jr. is a native of Washington D.C. and is a featured speaker with the National Christian Youth Speakers Network. Frank is married to the former Julie Vance and they reside in Waldorf, Maryland with their baby, Hannah Grace. Frank works full-time on Capitol Hill with the Republican National Committee and speaks across America at churches, revivals, youth rallies, school assemblies, leadership conferences, colleges and convocations.

Frank attended the Billy Graham School of Evangelism and was a youth pastor at three churches and the Minister of Evangelism at Dunkirk Baptist Church. His mission is to "Know God and make God known." He has a gift to "reach the un-reached" and his passion is encouraging discouraged people. He is the founder of the largest annual Christian Youth Rally in Southern Maryland and he uses humor, impersonations and incredible stories that Exalt the Savior, Encourage the Saints, Evangelize the Sinner and remind adults and adolescents to Expect the Son (because Jesus is coming back)!" For booking: "Frankly Speaking: Frank Shelton Ministries, P.O. Box 742, Waldorf, Maryland, 20604 (301) 843-3773 visit: www.frankshelton.com

Some of Frank's Topics: Abstinence, Attitude determines your Altitude, Character Counts, Leadership, Overcoming Obstacles, Power of Prayer, Are you WAITING on the Lord or is the Lord waiting on you? Giving God ALL you Got, JOY: Jesus first, Others second and Yourself last.

Josh Shipp

20-year-old Josh Shipp is a national youth motivator, humorist, and enthusiast! This goofy and dynamic young man has shared his inspiring message with over 200,000 people in 1999-2000 alone and has shared the stage with speakers such as comedian Bill Cosby. Josh's personal message of triumph over tragedy motivates youth to overcome life struggles and to live life to the fullest. Josh will have your audience dancing in the isles, laughing hysterically, chanting leadership phrases, and most importantly believing in themselves.

Josh Shipp
7242 N.W. 36th #235
Bethany, Oklahoma 73008
www.JoshShipp.com
Toll Free: (877) 582-6898

Order Copies of this Book for Your Next Event!

1 -99 - $10.00 each
100 - 999 - $9.00 each
1000 – 2,999 - $7.50 each
3000 – plus - $6.00 each
* Minumum order 25 books
*You will be invoiced for your order.
* Shipping & Handling charges will be included:

Number of Books:_____
Total Investment:_____
Make checks payable to:
Sam Glenn, Motivational Presentations

Name:_____
Organization:_____
Street Address:_____
City:_____St:_____Zip:_____
Phone:_____
Fax:_____
E-mail:_____

3 Ways to Order this Book!

* Consider passing this book out to youth at your next event!

1.   Phone : Call **800-818-6378**

2.   Website: **samglenn.com**

3.   Mail:

> Sam Glenn, Motivational Presentations
> 608 S Washington Ste 101
> Naperville, IL 60450